I did tell,
I did

I did tell, I did

The True Story of a Little Girl Betrayed By Those Who Should Have Loved Her

CASSIE HARTE

This book is based on the author's experiences. In order to protect
privacy, some names, identifying characteristics, dialogue and
details have been changed or reconstructed.

HarperElement
An Imprint of HarperCollins*Publishers*
77–85 Fulham Palace Road,
Hammersmith, London W6 8JB

www.harpercollins.co.uk

and *HarperElement* are trademarks
of HarperCollins*Publishers* Ltd

First published by HarperElement 2009

7

A catalogue record of this book is
available from the British Library

ISBN 978-0-00-733088-1

Printed and bound in Great Britain by
Clays Ltd, St Ives plc

For every child who has suffered abuse in silence and every adult who has had the courage to tell.

Foreword

There was never a time in my life when I wasn't lonely and afraid. Right back as a toddler I already knew I was different, the odd one out, the reason for all the conflict in our family. I knew because I was told that every single day.

'I never wanted to have you,' Mum said constantly. 'You've ruined my life. You spoiled everything, you did.'

Anything that went wrong or got broken was my fault. Every day she told me I was getting under her feet, driving her mad, making her ill. Her life would have been so much better if I had never been born. My sisters and brother were blameless but I was the troublemaker, the source of all the family's problems.

When you are told often enough that you're plain and worthless, stupid and a liar, you believe it's true. What was wrong with me? Why was I so rotten and bad? I was only a little girl, trying her hardest to please, trying her best to make her mother love her.

I did tell, I did

If you think you're worthless, you don't stand up for yourself in life, don't make any demands. You believe you deserve no better. So when there is a bad person, an evil person, around, then you're really in trouble. There's no one to turn to and nowhere you'll be safe. Evil people target the vulnerable; they can sniff them out.

Right through my childhood and into my twenties, I was never protected, never safe. Most children run to their mothers when they are scared and unhappy or when something unspeakable happens to them. For me, that was never going to work. I was unwanted. Unloved. Completely alone.

I did tell,
I did

Chapter One

My sister Ellen was ten when I was born and Rosie was eight, while my brother Tom was only two. Ellen was special because she was the first-born, while Rosie had been very ill as a baby and suffered learning difficulties as a result, meaning she was cosseted by all and sundry. Tom was Mum's favourite, her 'precious pup' who never put a foot wrong as far as she was concerned. And then there was me, Cassie, otherwise known as 'Plain Jane', with my long, dark curly hair, much darker than any of the others.

I was never in any doubt about my position at the bottom of the heap in the family, as Mum never missed a chance to make it clear to me. When my nan came to visit on Sundays, we would have afternoon tea of ham and salad followed by fairy cakes with different-coloured icing, and I was always the last to get a cake. Everyone else was allowed to choose: Tom would go first, and he took the chocolate one; then my nana would go next, then Ellen and Rosie, and when there were two cakes left on the plate, Mum would take one and I'd be left with the last cake that no one else wanted. So I knew exactly where I stood in the pecking order. There was no question about that.

Everything that went wrong in the house was my fault: if there was mud on the carpet or a broken plate, I got the blame. When the doll's house furniture got left out on the floor and Mum accidentally stood on it, it was me she shouted at.

'It wasn't me,' I protested, tears springing to my eyes. 'I didn't do it.' I knew I hadn't because I'd been at my dance class that morning, and it had definitely been put away before I went to bed the night before. Ellen and Rosie played with it as well. Why didn't they get the blame?

'Liar!' Mum yelled. 'You're always telling lies. I don't know why I have to put up with this. My life would have been so different if only you hadn't been born.'

There was no point arguing. She had spoken and that was that.

When our cat was allowed to escape out the back door just before Mum was due to take him to the vet's, once again it was my fault.

'You stupid girl!' Mum screamed at me, utterly furious. 'I'll never catch him now.'

I knew it hadn't been me because I'd been in the back bedroom the whole time rubbing milk on the patent leather of my tap shoes until they shone, and cleaning the soles of my ballet shoes with chalky stuff so they didn't slip.

'That's it!' Mum decreed. 'You're not going to your dance class until you find the cat.'

When you are blamed for things you haven't done quite so often, you stop protesting after a while. I went out into the cold and searched for hours until I found the cat hiding in an outhouse, safe and sound, but I was too late for my class by then. I supposed it must somehow have been my fault after all, but I didn't know how.

Dance classes were my favourite thing in the world in my pre-school years. I'd been going from the age of two and I think I was quite good. Certainly, I could walk right on the tips of my toes and I always got a part in the concerts they gave. Once I played Little Bo Peep. My hair was already curly but Mum decided I needed to have ringlets for the role so she yanked my hair tight and tied it up with knots of rags on which I had to sleep the night before the show. She yanked my hair a lot, in fact. Long curly hair was the perfect thing for her to vent her frustrations on and my hair would often be tugged if I stood too close to her.

It sometimes seemed as though my siblings were living a different life than me, even though we were all in the same family. Mum used to take Tom and my sisters out shopping and they'd come home laden with new toys and clothes, but she never bought anything new for me. They went for picnics and fun day trips, while I was left behind with Mrs Rogers, the next-door neighbour. I accepted this because I had never known any different, but it made me very confused. Why did Mum cuddle them and not me? Why was I unwanted, unloved? I craved her love and approval, but no matter how hard I tried I could never get it.

I did tell, I did

Mum was a big, dark-haired woman – 'handsome', I heard my nan calling her. She was a very powerful character, physically and mentally strong, and used to getting her own way in life; you would probably describe her as a bit of a battleaxe. My dad, in contrast, was tall, thin and placid, a kind man who was no match for her. Like me, he was used to getting the rough edge of her tongue and he'd slink off to his shed in the back garden and shut the door, looking for a few hours of peace and quiet.

I was born in November 1945, while Dad was still stationed in Burma, where he'd been fighting with the Marines. He didn't come home until I was six months old, then he went away again on and off for the next few years, and when he came back to live with us for good he got a job as a shipbuilder in the dock-yard near where we lived. He cycled to and from work and I remember him always arriving home cold, wet and tired after a long hard day. Every Friday lunchtime, in the years before I started school, I'd accompany Mum to the dockyard gate where she'd take his pay packet off him as soon as he was paid. Mum would count the notes and coins carefully into her purse, then give him back just enough to buy his cigarettes for the week. The rest was for the housekeeping.

We lived in a bungalow with a little garden out the back and a concrete patio. It wasn't very big – there were only two bedrooms – and when I was little, all four of us kids top-and-tailed in the one bed. Tom and I would have our heads at the bottom, while Ellen and Rosie's heads were at the headboard, and Ellen used to read us bedtime stories every night. We kept our books under the bed. One night she asked for another book and I stretched my hand under the bed to get one and felt something tickly running over me. I looked down and let out a piercing shriek because the biggest spider I had ever seen was scurrying across the floor.

We all jumped out of bed and ran out of the house screaming hysterically, whereupon the man next door came out to see what was going on. When we told him, he found a jam jar and went into our house to catch the spider, because it seemed the man down the road had lost his pet spider earlier that week. I think it might have been a tarantula or something.

Ellen and Rosie were often left to babysit for us in the days when Dad was still on assignment with the Marines because Mum liked to go out in the evening. Shortly after we'd had our tea, she would put on her best clothes and re-do her makeup, then she'd slip out the door in a cloud of perfume, instructing us to do whatever Ellen told us. But being looked after by my sisters wasn't a problem for me. I didn't mind at all because they were nice to me – much nicer than Mum would have been – and usually Tom and I would fall asleep to the sound of Ellen reading us a story. If Mum were at home, I'd probably be in trouble for something or other and sent up to bed on my own with her cruel words ringing in my ears, sometimes rubbing my cheek where a stinging slap had been delivered.

One battleground was at mealtimes. I was a small child, tiny for my age. 'If there's a puff of wind, it will knock you over,' my nan used to say. 'You don't eat enough to keep a sparrow alive.' I never had a big appetite but I particularly hated green vegetables. Sprouts were the worst as they made me feel physically sick. Every Sunday, Mum would make a roast and serve it with sprouts or great piles of over-boiled cabbage, then make me sit there until my plateful was all finished. It wasn't fair because Tom and my sisters never had to eat their greens. They chose what they wanted and left the table when they'd had enough, whether they'd cleaned their plates or not. I would sit staring at my soggy vegetables, willing myself to eat it all, but I would start to retch as soon as I raised the fork to my mouth. I just couldn't do it.

Mum would keep on at me: 'You're not leaving that table till you've eaten the lot,' she'd say unkindly, seeming to enjoy my suffering.

I started going to Sunday school at the age of three. We would draw pictures of bible stories and collect little cards to stick in an album, and I loved it, but often I had to miss it because I hadn't finished my vegetables at dinner. I'd sit there all afternoon, by which stage the vegetables were cold and greasy with fat from the roast. I wasn't even allowed to go to the toilet, so I became increasingly uncomfortable, crossing my legs to stop me from wetting myself. I could hear my brother and sisters playing in the next room or out in the garden but still I sat locked in this showdown that Mum was never going to let me win.

Teatime came, and I wasn't allowed any of the meal the others were having until I had eaten my sprouts.

'You're ruining the day for everyone else,' she accused me. 'Do you think I want to be here nagging you all afternoon? Do you think I haven't got better things to do?'

Eventually I would give in and choke down the mound of green sludge on my plate. I was then excused and more often than not I had to run straight to the bathroom to throw up. After that, I'd be ordered to sit in the bedroom on my own all evening.

I kept hoping that she would realise how ill this made me and relent. I never lost the hope that one day she might think I wasn't such a bad girl after all, and that maybe she could love me the way she loved my brother and sisters. Oh, how I hoped! But at Sunday lunch I could never stop myself from glancing over at my brother's and sisters' plates and wondering why it was so important that I ate my greens while they didn't. What was the difference between us?

I loved Tom and looked up to him, and used to hang around him trying to copy whatever he did. In my little girl's head, I reasoned that if I did what he was doing, surely Mum wouldn't have any reason to be nasty to me? She was never nasty to him. But sadly it didn't work that way, and I couldn't understand why. What was I doing wrong?

Most little girls have hugs and love, are told they are princesses and that they are treasured. All the love they need, they are given by the person whose love they should have by rights – their mother's. But I knew from an early age that my mother never wanted me and, consequently, never loved me. I didn't feel anyone loved me – whatever love meant.

One of the earliest memories I have is of some huge stone steps in front of an official-looking building. I must have been three or four at the time. Years later I realised that these stone

I did tell, I did

steps led up to the Guildhall, the home to what was then called the Welfare department, and is now Social Services. We climbed these steps and went in. Mum talked to the receptionist first, then a lady in a tweed suit came out, holding a booklet in her hand.

'Here's the child,' Mum said. 'She's all yours. I don't want her so it's up to you lot to take care of her.'

I looked around. Did she mean me? There was no other child in sight.

'We can't take a child just like that. That's not how it works,' the lady said, sounding very surprised.

Take me where? No one had said I was going anywhere. What did she mean?

Mum suddenly turned and hurried off down the steps, leaving me behind. 'I'm not having her back,' she shouted. 'I've brought her here to you and it's your job to take her off my hands.'

I stood in shock and confusion, my face burning bright red. The woman in the tweed suit kept arguing with Mum and I stared at the ground. Life was already scary for me at home because I knew Mum hated me, but she was the only mother I had, the only little bit of security. What would happen to me if I were left with the lady in the tweed suit? Would *she* look after me then? There was a loud rushing sound in my ears so I didn't hear everything that was said, but eventually Mum must have caved in.

She charged back up the steps, grabbed me by the arm and yanked me towards her. That's when I started crying, because she really hurt my arm. It felt as though she was nearly pulling it out of its socket.

'I'll be back!' Mum yelled over her shoulder. 'Either that or I'll find some other way. I don't want her!'

All the way home, she berated me. 'You're nothing but a nuisance, always getting under my feet. What did I do to deserve the trouble you bring?'

When we got home I was sent to my room. Tom and my sisters were out at school and I couldn't wait for them to return because I felt so lonely. Why didn't Mum want me? I was her little girl. Was this normal? Did other mothers not want their children as well? How could a real mother say that to her daughter?

From my storybooks, I'd heard about wicked stepmothers, and I began to fantasise that maybe Mum wasn't my real mother. Maybe my real mum was out there somewhere and one day she would turn up and take me away to live with her. She would love me and be nice to me and not shout at me the whole time. She would certainly never call me Plain Jane and tell me that I'd ruined her life.

There were some people in my young life who were kind to me. My two nans – Dad's mum, who I called Nana B, and Mum's mum, Nana C – were both nice people. We saw Nana C every weekend, Nana B less frequently. I got the impression that there had been some kind of falling out between Mum and Nana B, because Mum was always very curt with her, but she was good to me when we saw her.

Nana B broke her leg when I was about three and Mum and I had to go out collecting rent for her round some houses that she owned. Mum was good at it because she was so fierce. I remember some people telling her that they didn't have the money and Mum crossed her arms and told them she would stand there all day until they gave it to her. I tried to hide behind her, upset and embarrassed that she was being rude to strangers, but she was in her element.

Nana C was a tiny lady, quite frail, but she was very kind and gentle with me when Mum wasn't looking. She told me about the dreams she had had when she was a little girl – dreams that unfortunately were never fulfilled. She'd always wanted to be a dancer, but after her mum died when she was very young she was put in a workhouse along with her sisters and two little brothers and the dancing dream came to an end. As soon as she was old enough to get a job, albeit a menial one, she took it to save enough money to get her brothers out of the workhouse. She continued to work until she met and married my granddad, so she never did get the chance to be a dancer. She told me that whatever happened I had to make sure I followed my own dreams so I would be happy.

Happy? What was that? I had no idea what she meant.

I think Nana C knew that Mum shouted at me a lot because she witnessed it on plenty of occasions, but she was always careful not to be too friendly to me when Mum was watching. It was as if she was scared of her own daughter.

Dad was the same. He was always lovely if I went out to visit him in his shed, where we'd have little chats on our own, but in front of Mum he would never dare stand up for me. He never stood up for himself either. No one stood up to Mum. It just wasn't worth it.

The other person who was nice to me was my godfather, a man I knew as Uncle Bill, although he wasn't a real uncle. He was always round the house in my younger years, before I went to school, and he'd make a huge fuss of me. Bill was tall, with jet black hair and twinkly eyes, and every time he came round he'd stop to give me a hug and tell me how much he loved me.

'How's my special girl today?' he'd ask, and I'd beam with pleasure. 'You've got such pretty hair, Cassie. What are you playing at today?'

He'd pull me onto his lap for a cuddle and I'd giggle in anticipation, knowing that his cuddles usually turned to tickles before long.

When Uncle Bill came to visit Mum at the house, I was often sent out into the garden to play for a while because they said they had grown-up business to discuss, but after they'd finished, Bill sometimes took me out. We'd have picnics together in the park, or he'd take me for a drive on his motorbike. He and Dad were both motorbike enthusiasts and our families would all meet up at rallies. Bill was married to a woman called Gwen, who was always nice to me when I saw her although I don't think she and Mum got on. I can't remember Gwen coming to the rallies very often, but when she did she would usually stand with my dad, or with her four sons, who were just a bit older than me.

One time Bill and I won a competition at a rally, where he was riding on his bike and I was sitting on the petrol tank holding an egg and spoon. It was the first thing I had ever won in my life and I was over the moon about it. The judges gave Uncle Bill a silver cup that gleamed in the sunshine and he handed it to me.

'I've got lots of cups at home, Cassie,' he smiled. 'You keep this one.'

It was quite heavy and I could hardly hold it, but I was so ecstatic to have this little bit of treasure that I struggled to keep it in my grasp. Then Mum saw it.

'Give that back straight away,' she hissed. 'You're not bringing that home. It's Bill's cup, not yours. You don't deserve it.'

And so I had no choice but to hand it over to Uncle Bill, all the while struggling to hold back my tears.

Every child needs to feel special to someone, and I knew I was special to Uncle Bill. He's the only person who ever hugged me as a child, or who told me that he loved me. He brought me presents – little things like new socks, my favourite sweetie cigarettes or a tiny bar of chocolate – and he took an interest in me. He kept telling me how clever I was, and what a great dancer, and he was always asking me to walk across the room on tippy-toes for him, or he'd put the radio on and ask me to do a little dance.

He was *my* godfather, *my* special uncle, and he paid attention to me rather than Tom or Ellen or Rosie. I felt proud when we rode off down the road on his bike with me balanced on the petrol tank. Proud that at least I had someone who cared about me, someone whose life I hadn't ruined by being born.

Chapter Two

When I was about four years old Ellen and Rosie went off to board in a Sunshine School. These were special schools for children who had suffered physical or emotional trauma during the war, and I assume they were sent there because of the trauma they'd experienced when Mum's house had been bombed. It was in a large naval port and had been hit twice, the second hit completely destroying it.

Although the age difference was too great for us to have been close, I really missed my sisters once they were gone. It was just Tom and me left in the house with Mum: Tom the favourite, and me the unloved, unwanted child. Dad came home from work late, and once Tom started school it was just Mum and me in the house during the day, and she hated that with a passion. It seemed I was always under her feet, no matter how hard I tried not to annoy her.

Every morning Mum used to make me sit and brush my hair a hundred times on each side. Of course, I couldn't count to a hundred in those days but I knew it was a big number and that I had to keep on brushing for ages until she said I could stop. One morning Mum had gone into the back garden and I could hear her chatting over the fence to Mrs Rogers, our neighbour. I sat in front of the electric bar heater, brushing and brushing, trying to make my hair gleam in the hope that Mum would be pleased with me.

Suddenly I heard a crackling noise and when I looked up into the mirror I saw flames shooting out from the side of my head. I rushed out into the garden screaming as loud as I could, 'Mum! Help!'

The flames flared up into a big bright mass as I reached the two women. Mrs Rogers had been hanging out her laundry and she quickly grabbed a wet towel from her basket and threw it over my head, putting the fire out. There was a sizzling noise and a strong smell of burning.

When Mum pulled the towel off, I was horrified to see that huge clumps of my hair were still in it, having come away from my scalp.

'You *stupid* girl!' Mum yelled, smacking me hard across the back of the head. 'You were sitting too close to the heater, weren't you?' She slapped my face. 'Look what you've done.'

Mrs Rogers was more sympathetic. 'Poor thing, you must have got such a fright.'

'Fright? I'll give her a fright!' Mum commented before saying to me, 'Get back inside and I'll deal with you in a minute.' She turned to our neighbour again. 'She's the blight of my life, that one. You've got no idea what I have to put up with from her.'

Back inside, she sat me on the tall kitchen stool and started roughly chopping the rest of my hair off with a big pair of scissors. I cried quietly to myself as she yanked my head to one side then the other, muttering the whole time: 'Stupid girl. Can't even be trusted to brush her own hair without causing trouble.'

Fortunately the flames hadn't burned my scalp, but my hair was so badly singed that Mum had to crop it close all over and I looked like a boy when she'd finished. When I peered in the mirror, I didn't recognise myself at first, and I was sad because Uncle Bill always told me I had such lovely hair. He wouldn't be saying that now. I was definitely Plain Jane.

Dad seemed really shocked when he got home. 'Did you need to cut it back so far, Kath?' he asked sadly.

'You didn't see the state of her!' Mum cried. 'She could have had the whole house up in flames.'

He backed down straight away. It was never worth his while getting into conflict with her because he couldn't win no matter what he said. Once, only once, do I remember Dad criticising Mum for the way she treated me.

'She's just a child,' he said. 'Why are you always picking on her?'

Mum was so shocked at this intervention that she was speechless for a minute, then she started screaming: 'How can you speak to me like that? You've got no idea what I have to put up with from her. You're out at work all day so you don't see the way she's always under my feet, always being a nuisance, constantly getting on my nerves. I turn round and there she is, in the way again. If I speak harshly to her some-times, I'm only doing it for her own good. She needs to learn.'

Dad opened his mouth to speak up in my defence again, when Mum suddenly collapsed dramatically on the floor with a crash.

'Kath, Kath my sweet, talk to me! Can you hear me?' Dad knelt down beside her but she remained still, her eyes closed.

I was overcome with guilt. It was my fault she had collapsed, because I was such a nuisance. I tried not to be, but somehow I couldn't help it. What if she died? It would be all because of me and I would go to Hell, which I had learned about at Sunday school.

'Help me get her to the bedroom, Cassie,' Dad said. 'You take her feet.'

Between us we managed to carry her through and lay her on the bed, and she began to murmur incoherently.

'I'm sorry, love, I didn't mean it,' Dad said. 'It was wrong of me to question your judgement. Of course you know best when it comes to the children.'

I was crying by this stage, petrified about what I had done. 'I'm sorry I made you ill, Mum. I didn't mean to upset you. I'm really, really sorry.'

She opened her eyes and pulled herself up in the bed a little bit, and I could swear she was half-smiling, as if pleased with herself. 'Could you get me a cup of tea, love?' she asked Dad in a weak voice, and he scurried off to obey. She looked at me coldly. 'That'll teach you,' she remarked. 'Now get out of my sight, and stay out.'

Another time when I had upset Mum and Dad dared to speak up in my defence, she actually disappeared and was missing for hours. Dad and I walked the streets, me in tears, asking everyone we met if they had seen her but no one had. Eventually we went home when it got dark and I was terrified that she had left us for good. She may not have loved me or been kind to me but she was the only mother I had and I needed her. Who else would look after me? After all, I was unlovable, wasn't I?

I was exhausted, my face tear-stained and eyes swollen with crying, when she finally walked in the door. Dad leapt to his feet straight away, full of apologies. 'I'm sorry, love, I don't know what I was thinking of. Are you all right? Can I get you anything?'

'Sorry, Mum,' I ventured timidly.

'Go to your room,' she snapped, pointing her finger, and I scurried off to the bedroom.

I couldn't sleep, though. I lay awake wondering why I always managed to upset Mum so badly. It must be my fault, because Tom never made her cross like that and I don't remember her ever raising her voice with my sisters. I tried my hardest to please her but nothing I did was good enough. No matter what I did, I couldn't make her love me the way she loved them. There must be something wrong with me, something horrible deep inside me that I couldn't change.

I was very shy and withdrawn in company and tried to keep myself to myself. That way, I reckoned, I wouldn't say the wrong thing and bring Mum's wrath down on my head – but it never worked. When Mum's friends came round and I hid in the corner, she would berate me for being rude and unsociable.

'You'll have to apologise next time they come round. I've never been so embarrassed in my life!' she would scold. 'Why do you always have to show me up?'

The harder I tried, it seemed, the less I got it right. Nothing I did would ever please Mum and, kind as he was, I couldn't rely on Dad to protect me because he wouldn't dare stand up to her.

The only respite came when Mum went into hospital for a while and Dad looked after us. She suffered from 'women's problems' and had to have several operations while I was young. She would leave orders and a strict regime for Dad to follow and he would always promise to obey to the letter, not wanting to upset her before she went into hospital. But once she was gone, the regime relaxed because he could never be as hard on me as she was.

I loved the mushy chips Dad made. He let the fat get so hot that the chips became all light and fluffy and delicious, and Tom and I both loved them. When Mum was back home recuperating, he made chips like this for her once and she was angry that they were mushy, so it became a special way that he made chips for us only when she was in hospital.

He also burned the milk accidentally when he was making custard once and I loved the flavour that way, so from then on he'd make burnt custard just for me – but only when Mum was in hospital.

On those days, he used to chat to Tom and me and ask us how we were, then he'd tuck us up in bed at night and give us a hug. Something my mother never did for me. Something that made me feel loved and safe. These were happy times. There weren't many of them. I thought of them as the 'in-between' times, when I felt safe and protected. Whenever Mum wasn't there.

The other happy thing in my life was my dancing. The dance school was a big deal in our area and I went twice a week, along with the girl next door. I absolutely loved the ballet teacher, Una, who was slim and elegant, and always wore her hair up in a French pleat at the back. One time I remember her unpleating it after class and I was astonished to see how long her hair was – right down to her waist.

I was never shy about performing in concerts because on stage I could pretend to be someone else – someone lovable, someone whose mother wanted her. Of course, Mum never came to my shows. Uncle Bill would turn up at the end to give me a lift home on the bike, and he'd shower me with praise and give me lots of cuddles but I'm not sure that he ever watched much of the show – or if he did, I never saw him. I would be looking out for Mum, and would always be disappointed when she wasn't there, so I suppose I stopped looking for anyone else.

Once, I was doing the Dance of the Cygnets in *Swan Lake*, which is very tricky to perform as you have to move sideways in a line exactly in time with the dancers next to you. At the end, Una came up to me and asked if my mother was there. I said no, she couldn't make it, so Una said she would come round the house to talk to her the next day.

Mum seemed surprised when Una turned up but led her into the front room. Dad and I trooped in as well and I sat on the floor by Dad's feet.

'You should have seen Cassie dancing last night,' Una began. 'She's very talented and I'm sure you'd have been proud of her.'

No, she wouldn't, I thought to myself.

'Anyway,' Una continued, 'I wondered if you would consider sending her to ballet school? I'm sure she would get a scholarship because she's got a very special gift. It would mean living away from home, of course …' Her voice tailed off at the look on Mum's face.

'That's ridiculous! She can't possibly be good enough,' Mum snapped.

'I assure you she is,' Una maintained.

'How can she be better than my other children? I'm not having her offered an opportunity that they never had. I won't hear of it!'

Una tried to argue but Mum had made up her mind and that was that.

I was bitterly disappointed. The thought of getting away from home, away from Mum's anger, was like a dream to me – but it wasn't to be. I would go to the local primary school where Tom was already a pupil and that was that. End of story.

In fact, I went to three different schools at the age of five because we moved home twice that year. I spent two terms in the local primary near the bungalow and, despite being shy, I loved it straight away. I made friends easily because I worked hard at getting people to like me. I was so keen to have friends that I went along with whatever games they wanted to play, just delighted to be allowed to be one of the crowd.

Then one evening when Tom and I got home from school, Dad came through to us.

'Do you hear that noise?' he asked. 'What do you think it is?'

We both listened and I heard a tiny, high-pitched wail.

'Is it a cat?' Tom asked, and Dad laughed.

'No, it's not a cat. It's a baby. A little baby girl. Do you want to come and see her?'

Mum was in bed and the baby was lying in a cot beside her. I fell in love the first time I looked at her little screwed-up face and her tiny hands, only slightly bigger than my doll's hands.

'She's called Anne,' Dad told us. 'Say hello to your new sister.'

I had always liked playing with dolls. I had a black doll of my own, called Suzie, and sometimes I would be allowed to play with my big sisters' dolls when they weren't around. But now I had a living, breathing doll to look after, and I thought that would be the best thing of all.

I couldn't stop looking at her and I'd creep into the room to watch her sleeping in her cot for ages, until Mum saw me.

'What do you think you're doing? Get away from her,' she'd snap. 'That's the last thing I need, you wakening her.'

Sometimes I'd ask timidly if I could pick her up or just touch her tiny fingers but Mum told me to keep my hands off her. Still, I'd risk her anger to sneak in and watch little Anne whenever I got the chance.

The bungalow was too small for all of us now. Shortly after Anne was born everything was packed up in boxes and we moved in with Nana B. It was a real crush. Tom and I slept on the floor and Anne had to sleep in a drawer because there wasn't any room for her cot. I had a few weeks at a school there that I didn't like very much at all – I suppose I never had a chance to get settled – then one night Mum and Nana B had a huge row. I don't know what it was about, but Mum bundled us all up and out into the streets, pushing baby Anne in her pram. Dad wasn't there that night. We walked for miles until we reached the beach.

'We'll have to sleep here,' Mum said.

'We can't,' Tom complained. 'It's dark and cold and I don't want to.'

'Just huddle up and we'll be fine,' Mum said.

A police car drew up at that point and a policeman jumped out. Mum burst into tears and complained that she didn't know what to do because her heartless mother-in-law had thrown her out on the streets with nowhere to go. I thought that was very odd, because I couldn't imagine Nana B throwing us out of her house. She'd always been very nice to Tom and me.

Anyway, the policeman found us a room in a big house where a kind lady brought us all hot chocolate to warm us up, then the next day we moved into a house on a council estate – a proper house, bigger than our bungalow, with an upstairs and a downstairs. I was quickly enrolled to start at the nearest primary school.

On the very first day there, I got chatting to a girl called Claire, a skinny girl with blonde curly hair who soon became my bestest friend in the world. We liked playing hopscotch and skipping together and we got on like a house on fire from the word go. It was the end of the school year shortly after I started and there was a school show, in which we both got parts. Claire was a Summer Fairy, dressed all in pink. I played a Red Goblin and then I had to do a quick change and be a fairy, and I remember I didn't have time to take my Red Goblin boots off so I went on in my fairy costume with these big clumpy boots and everyone laughed. I'd had to give up dancing classes when we moved from the bungalow, but being in a show like that made up for it a little bit.

Claire lived just round the corner from me so before long she took me home and introduced me to her mum and dad, who were the nicest people I'd ever met. Straight away they treated me like another member of their family. Whenever they were going on a family outing, I would be invited along with them. Sometimes Mum wouldn't let me go, just because she didn't want me to be having fun, but most of the time she agreed because, she said, she wanted to get me out from under her feet.

One day that summer we went to a holiday camp in Bognor Regis for the day. There was a big park with giant statues of nursery rhyme characters and we had our photos taken in front of them. There was a huge cup and saucer, part of the *Alice in Wonderland* tea party, and Claire's dad took a picture of the two of us sitting inside the cup. It was a lovely, magical place. I'd never been anywhere like it in my life before. After we had explored it from end to end, we went down to the beach and played ball on the sand. The whole day stands out for me as one of the best days of my entire childhood.

All my clothes and shoes were hand-me-downs from Ellen and Rosie, and nothing ever fitted me properly. I'd have to stuff newspaper in the toes of the shoes and pin up hems so I didn't trip over them. Tom and the girls got new outfits whenever they needed them but Mum never bought me anything new.

One day, in our second year at primary school, Claire and I were invited to the birthday party of another friend of ours. I dressed up in the best hand-me-down frock I could find and set off to pick up Claire at her house. She answered the door holding a lovely blue flowered dress.

'Do you like it?' she asked, excited. 'Do you like the colour?'

'It's beautiful. I love it,' I told her.

She giggled. 'Well, you can have it then.'

I was confused. 'I can't just take your dress. It's yours.'

'No, it's not,' she laughed. 'Mum bought it for you. I have the same dress in pink!'

She led me to her room and there was another dress laid out on the bed. We hugged each other and danced round the room, excited to have brand new matching dresses, but a bit of me felt odd about it. Why should Claire's mum buy me a new dress? Why didn't my own mum do that?

She popped her head round the door. 'Are you girls all right?' she asked. 'Do you like your new dress, Cassie?'

'I love it. Thank you so much,' I said, embarrassed.

'I just thought it would be nice for you and Claire to be twins for the party,' she said gaily. 'Your mum must have her hands full with the new baby and she probably doesn't have time to go shopping for you at the moment. I noticed your clothes were looking a bit worn.'

I blushed, and didn't tell her that it wasn't just since the new baby – that Mum had never bought me any new clothes. From then on, whenever Claire got a new dress, her mum bought a matching one for me as well. How good was that? How kind they were. I felt so lucky! I would always leave the clothes she bought for me at their house, though. If I had taken them home, I don't think Mum would have let me keep them. It felt as though Claire and I were sisters. I often wished that we could have been, so that I could move into her house and stay there instead of having to go back to live in our house with a mother who hated me.

The more I saw of Claire's family life, the more I realised how odd my own family was. What mother calls her daughter 'Plain Jane' and tells her she isn't wanted? The times I spent with Claire and her family allowed me to daydream that I belonged there. I tried to pretend that her mum and dad were mine, that I was one of them and that they loved me. I could be happy imagining that I was part of their family, until it was time to go home and reality reared its ugly head again.

Uncle Bill still came to visit regularly once we were in the new house. Mum looked forward to him coming round and she would always fix her lipstick and clear the baby's nappies from the rail where they were drying in front of the fire in the back room. She seemed more cheerful when he was there and she never shouted at me in front of him – but she did plenty of shouting before he arrived.

After I'd set my hair on fire and Mum chopped it all off, it had grown back straight and this seemed to make her very cross. 'Bill loved your curls,' she said. 'You always have to ruin everything!' So before he came round, I'd have to sit having my hair curled with metal tongs that she heated in the gas flame on the cooker. Many a time she would burn my forehead or neck with them but if I screamed she would slap me, so I learned just to shut my eyes and bite my lip.

Uncle Bill would arrive and it would be all cuddles and hugs and praise and presents. At home, they were the only shows of affection I had ever received. However, he got a bit jealous once I started spending my free time over at Claire's. He didn't seem to like that.

'You're always over there now,' he complained next time he saw me. 'Your poor old Uncle Bill misses you.'

He grabbed me for a hug and kiss and his chin scratched my cheek. I tried to pull away but he turned the hug into a tickle. I wriggled and squirmed but he pulled me down onto the sofa and kept tickling me all over until I thought I was going to wet myself.

'Let go!' I whimpered. 'Please.'

'I'm going to teach you a lesson,' he said. 'I'm going to tickle you until you promise you'll definitely be here next time I come.'

His fingers were everywhere – in my ribs, under my arms, my legs, my tummy.

'I promise,' I gasped. 'I promise.' I kept repeating it, until he eventually let me go.

I felt a bit strange afterwards. A bit uneasy. I couldn't explain it any more clearly than that. It didn't feel wrong, but it didn't feel right either.

One day soon after that, when I was sitting on Uncle Bill's lap in the best room, things definitely started to feel wrong. Some friends of Mum's had come to visit, and as they sat chatting I felt a movement under my skirt. It felt as though something was trying to get in between my legs. I wriggled and Uncle Bill laughed and held me closer. That's when I realised that he had his hand underneath me and was rubbing at the top of my thigh.

'No,' I said quietly and tried to get off. 'Don't.'

He laughed and lifted me up, walking towards the door. 'I think she's getting bored,' he said to the ladies. 'I'll take her outside to play.'

He carried me out into the garden and, as he set me down, he slid his hand up my skirt and inside my panties onto my bottom. I didn't like it. I felt that it was wrong. I wriggled to get away, and he laughed.

'Never mind,' he said. 'We'll play another time.'

Play? I didn't think I liked this kind of 'play'. Claire's dad often played with us, chasing us up and down the stairs, or playing catch in the garden. He would sometimes throw us up into the air, or give us a hug and a goodnight kiss on the cheek. This kind of 'play' was good and never made me feel uneasy.

I did tell, I did

I began to feel less comfortable around Uncle Bill after that. Next time he came round I eyed him warily, trying to stay at arm's length. I still wanted to be his favourite girl – needed to be – but I didn't always like his kind of games. They made me feel funny. He was still the kind uncle who brought me presents and said he loved me but I wasn't so relaxed when he was around. I wished with all my heart that we could just go back to the way things were before. Before he started wanting to 'play' with me.

Chapter Three

At home, Mum gave me the hardest chores to do round the house. Tom would occasionally be asked to dry the dishes after dinner, but I was the one who had the tough jobs: I had to scrub the wooden draining boards with a scrubbing brush and carbolic soap that left my hands raw; polish the front steps with Cardinal red polish, which I had to be careful not to smudge onto the path; and squeeze the washing through the huge mangle, which was much bigger than I was. These jobs were physically tough for me, but I had no choice. If I argued about the unfairness, I would be punished for daring to question her.

One day, when I was pushing a sheet through the roller of the mangle, it got stuck. 'I can't do this, it's too hard for me,' I called to Mum.

She came out and I thought at first that she was going to help me, but she angrily grabbed the wheel that turned the rollers and yanked it round before I had a chance to move my hand.

I screamed 'Stop! Stop!' as my hand began to disappear between the huge rollers. She stopped the wheel and wrenched my arm hard, releasing my squashed fingers. The pain was awful and I couldn't stop crying, holding my crushed hand to my mouth. Suddenly I felt a slap across my face.

'You stupid girl – look what you've done now.' She pointed to the sheet that was now tangled between the rollers. 'How am I supposed to get that out?'

She ordered me back into the house and I ran up to my bedroom and cried.

I didn't resent having to do all the hard work while Tom sat and played, but it did occasionally make me feel like Cinderella. Except that I didn't go to the ball, I didn't meet my prince, and he didn't whisk me away.

In our free time, Tom and I had fun together. I would tag along with him wherever he went and he never seemed to mind. He bossed me around a bit but I was happy to be his slave if he would just love me in return. I'd have done virtually anything he told me to do as a youngster.

When I was five, and we were both at the same infant's school, he called me over while I was standing in the dinner queue and told me that it was home time. I was confused, as all the other children were queuing to go in and have their dinner. But Tom insisted that we had to go home because school was over for the day.

I believed him. I would have believed anything he said. He was my idol. We left the school together, my brother and I. Once out and running along the pavement, he admitted that I was right, that it was dinner time not home time, but he said that he didn't want to stay in school and it would be OK because I was with him. So I believed that it was OK. If he said it was OK, then it was.

We went into an orchard where he told me we were allowed to pick fruit. Again I believed him. We 'scrumped' plums and apples, eating them as we went round. It was fun, climbing trees and throwing fruit at each other. An adventure. An in-between time.

At the end of the afternoon we left the orchard and I remember feeling quite poorly. My tummy hurt and we sat down on the kerb. Unfortunately, we were spotted by a friend of our mother's. She asked us why we weren't at school and, quick as a flash, my brother told her that we had a dental appointment and were late. We scurried off.

We might have got away with it, except that this woman was about to visit our house. When we got home later, our formidable mother was waiting, arms folded, at the front door.

'Where the hell do you think you've been?' she screamed at me, clipping me round the ear. 'Get to your room.'

'My stomach hurts,' Tom moaned, bending over and clutching at it.

'See what you've done? You've made your brother ill. Now, get out of my sight!'

In my head I was protesting: 'He told me it was okay. He said we were allowed. It's not fair. My tummy hurts too.' But out loud I didn't say anything. Whatever scrapes Tom got me into, I loved him anyway and I would never do anything to hurt him.

I don't remember Mum ever hitting Tom, but she hit me. She was a big woman and she'd slap me so hard that it sent me flying across the room. I once lost a hank of hair where she grabbed hold of it and pushed me against a wall, and the handful came clean out of my scalp.

The physical pain wasn't the problem, though. It was the emotional pain. I was desperate for her to love me, dying to find a way to win her affection. As soon as I could write, I started writing her poems and notes telling her I loved her. I used to slip them into the drawer where she kept all her letters, thinking she would find them and be touched by them, but she never mentioned that she'd seen them. Sometimes I would be too afraid to give them to her so I kept them in a scrapbook under my bed. I hoped one day that she would change and show she loved me, then I would give her all these secret things. I made presents for her as well, or drew pictures, but more often than not if I handed them over she dumped them straight in the bin. I tiptoed around, trying my hardest to please her, but nothing I could do was right.

I could never understand why I annoyed Mum so much, but I was always looking for clues, and one day, when I was six years old, I overheard her chatting to a friend of hers we called Auntie Prue. Normally I was sent out into the garden or up to my room when she had company – 'Get out of my sight and stay out!' – but on this particular occasion she'd sent me into the kitchen to lay out a tray of tea and biscuits. As I walked back through the hall with it, I heard Auntie Prue mentioning my name and I stopped for a moment.

'She was a mistake. A very unfortunate mistake. Having her ruined my life,' Mum said passionately.

I must have made a sound in the hall – an intake of breath maybe – because Mum realised I was standing there listening. She jumped to her feet, took the tray from me and placed it on the table, then grabbed me by the hair.

'You're the reason for all the unhappiness in our family,' she screamed. 'You know that, don't you?' As she shouted, she dragged me by the hair to the back door and threw me out into the garden.

I huddled down, sobbing and trying to work out what she could possibly have meant. In what way was I a mistake? Did that mean she hadn't meant to have me? I didn't know where babies came from but I assumed you had to ask for them in some way, that they didn't just come uninvited.

My Nana C had been an assistant midwife and she used to talk about 'bringing babies into the world'. As a child I thought that perhaps there was a door somewhere and Nana C opened it and brought in a baby. That's how naïve I was. I guessed that maybe the midwife who brought me had picked up the wrong baby by mistake. Was that what Mum meant? When Anne was born, Mum had been delighted with her, and still was. She must have been the right baby. She wasn't a mistake. It was just me. I was the problem.

After a while I heard Mum going out, so I crept back into the house and ran up to the bathroom and locked the door, shaking, scared and confused. I'd been in there for quite some time when I heard footsteps approaching up the stairs and then Uncle Bill calling my name.

'Cassie? Where are you, sweetheart?' He tried the bathroom door and, realising it was locked, sat down to talk to me through it.

'Mum doesn't love me,' I sobbed. 'She said I was an unfortunate mistake. She says I ruined her life.'

'Don't you worry,' he soothed. 'She doesn't mean it. Anyway, you've got me and I love you. I'll look after you.'

No one else had ever told me they loved me before – not Dad, or Tom, or my sisters, and certainly not Mum. The only affection I ever got was from Uncle Bill, and no matter how uneasy I had felt that day in the garden, I desperately needed his love. Eventually I unlocked the door and came out, and he gave me a great big hug, which brought on a fresh wave of sobbing.

My mother came back at that point. 'Is she still creating?' she shouted up the stairs. 'Why don't you take her out for a drive to calm her down and get her out of my hair?'

I thought anything was better than staying in the house with her, so I got my cardy and followed him out to the car, holding his hand trustingly.

Uncle Bill was very proud of his car – a black Austin. He was the first person in the neighbourhood to get a car and he never missed a chance to be seen out and about in it. I felt special sitting on the front seat with him, gazing out the window, breathing in the leathery, petrolly smell.

We drove out to the countryside, to a lovely spot that he knew I liked, high up on a hill with a view over the sprawling city below. It was a perfect sunny day and Uncle Bill had brought a picnic with him, of biscuits, fruit and orange squash.

He also had a packet of sweetie cigarettes, my favourites. He spread out a rug to sit on and we ate first, then we played ball and chased butterflies and picked wildflowers. I felt loved, safe and special. After all the earlier emotional turmoil, I felt happy again so I was sorry when the day came to an end and it was time to get back in the car and head home.

Uncle Bill put his arm round me. 'Let's get into the back for a cuddle. That will end the day nicely,' he said.

I had no reason to be afraid after such a lovely, happy afternoon so I clambered into the back of his car and he wrapped his arms round me and held me tightly. But then he started to kiss my face roughly, in a way that he had never done before, and when I tried to pull away he held my head so I couldn't move it. Next his hands started to touch me all over – on my back, my bottom, then between my legs – and I knew instinctively it was wrong.

'No, you're hurting me,' I cried. 'Please don't do this. Please stop.'

It was as if he didn't hear me. He was a big man, a strong man, and all my pushing him away made no difference. He was still professing his love for me but at the same time he was hurting me, his big rough hands gripping my skinny little body, his fingers poking me inside my panties. I was terrified.

'Please stop, please don't do this.' I began to cry.

He seemed shaken by my tears and at last he pulled away. 'All right, all right, I'll take you home,' he snapped, sounding cross. He clambered into the front seat, then turned to me with a nasty tone. 'You can't tell anyone about this, do you hear?

You can't tell what happened because if you do they'll blame you.'

I was confused. How could this be my fault? What had I done to deserve this?

And then to make things even worse, he continued, 'If you say that I hurt you and made you cry, they won't believe you.' He laughed. 'After all, did I make you climb into the back of the car?'

I was shaking with fear. Why had he done that? Where was the nice uncle who said he loved me? He shouldn't have done that.

We drove home in silence. I couldn't understand how he could have hurt me this way. He loved me, didn't he? Everything was confusing.

As soon as we got home I ran up to the safety of the bathroom. I felt dirty and sore between my legs so I stood in the bath and scrubbed myself with hot, soapy water. It began to sting but I kept scrubbing because I wanted to make what had happened go away. I felt bruised all over where his big fingers had gripped me so tightly, but worse than the physical pain was the terrible loneliness and fear. Who could I turn to now? How could I ever feel safe again? I had no one left on my side. When I had finished washing, I took myself to bed and cried until I was so exhausted that I finally fell asleep.

Shortly after this, Mum announced at breakfast one Saturday that Uncle Bill was going to spend the day with me. My sisters had returned from boarding school a few weeks before and they were taking Tom to a pantomime – a family treat that of course I wasn't included in – while Mum and Dad were going shopping.

'I'll be OK in the house on my own,' I said quickly, terrified that the things that had happened in the car might happen again.

'Don't be so ungrateful,' my mother snapped. 'You're staying with Bill and that's that.'

When he arrived, grinning from ear to ear, I couldn't bear to look at him. As soon as Mum and Dad left, I told him I wanted to go out and play with a friend, but he wasn't about to let me do that.

'We can play together,' he said. 'It'll be fun.'

I was almost shaking with fear. I didn't want this *fun*. I felt betrayed by him. He was the one person who I thought cared about me and yet he could still hurt me like that.

He walked across the room smiling. 'Come on, you know you like it. I'll make you feel really good.'

Like it? Feel good? How could he think that when I'd told him he had hurt me? Why would I like that?

He put his arm around me and pulled me down to the floor then he held me with one arm and started kissing me all over my face, scratching me with his bristly chin. The floor was hard and hurting my back. He pulled my hand and pressed it against the front of his trousers, forcing me to touch him.

'No!' I cried, trying to wriggle away. 'Please! Please don't hurt me again.'

He wasn't listening. He just carried on moaning and slobbering over me. It was horrible and I knew I couldn't let it happen.

I did tell, I did

I managed to wrench my hand out of his grip and tried to push him away but he was very strong. With his free hand he had lifted my skirt and was pulling at my panties, trying to touch my shaking body. He opened the top of his trousers and his *awfulness* was showing.

What was he doing? What was happening? Surely he shouldn't be doing that to me, should he?

Summoning all the strength I possessed, I struggled out from under him and made a bolt for the stairs. In complete panic, I raced up to the bathroom and locked the door behind me, then I sank down on the floor sobbing uncontrollably.

Was I safe? Would he break the door down? How would he explain the situation when Mum and Dad came home?

'Come on, Cassie, don't be silly,' Uncle Bill coaxed through the door. 'What's the matter with you? It's just a harmless bit of fun.'

But I wouldn't come out.

His tone changed. 'You can't ever tell anyone, you know. They won't believe you. They might even take you away to a children's home. That's where they put all the naughty boys and girls. In children's homes everyone would want to do things with you, they'd all be trying to kiss and cuddle you. Why don't you come out now and we can do something else instead? Would you like to play ball in the garden?'

But I wouldn't come out, wouldn't even speak to him, I was so traumatised by what had happened. Eventually he gave up trying to coax me and went back downstairs, but still I stayed huddled behind the locked door until my parents came home.

When they got back, I heard the adults talking downstairs but couldn't make out what was being said, then I heard my mother's footsteps clumping up the stairs.

'Come out right now,' she ordered. 'What do you think you're playing at?'

I unlocked the door and faced her, my eyes red and swollen from crying.

'Get into your bedroom,' she said, frowning and pushing me towards my room, 'so you can tell me what's been going on.'

I followed her through, shaking with fear.

She sat down on the bed and raised an eyebrow. 'So? Why have you been so rude to Bill?'

I stumbled as I tried to get the words out. 'He kissed me, Mum, and it hurt. He hurt me. I don't like him kissing me. It's horrible. And he touched me there.' I pointed between my legs. 'In my panties. And he made me touch him, and I don't want to do it any more. I don't like kisses and cuddles with him.' I was crying and stuttering and I think I was still shaking with the shock of the whole thing.

Mum listened calmly. She didn't seem at all angry or surprised. When I'd finished, she got up and left the room without saying a word to me and I heard her going downstairs.

Everything would be OK now. Mum would stop it from happening to me ever again. She had to, didn't she? Mums had to protect their little girls.

I heard raised voices downstairs and crept out onto the landing to listen. Dad sounded angry but I couldn't hear what he was saying. Surely he and Mum would make sure that Bill never came back to the house, even though he was my godfather?

Suddenly the living room door opened and Bill and my Mum appeared in the hall. They didn't see me watching from above.

'You don't believe any of this, do you?' Bill asked her. 'You don't believe I would ever do anything to hurt her?'

And then something happened that shattered my world. Mum leaned forward and kissed him on the lips. The man who had hurt me, her own little girl, so badly.

'Of course I don't believe her,' she said. 'She's a liar. Perhaps you should stay away for a while until things cool down, and I'll make sure she never says anything like this again. She won't dare!'

I didn't understand. Why would she say that? I was telling the truth. I didn't lie. But if my own mother didn't believe me, who would? Why would I make up something like that? I thought Uncle Bill had loved me. I wanted him to love me. I didn't want any of this to have happened.

After Bill left, Mum called me downstairs and I stood in front of her feeling very frightened and confused. I thought at first that she was going to try and explain my uncle's actions or reassure me that he would no longer be welcome at her house, but how wrong I was.

'How could you be so wicked?' she screamed. 'How could you tell such lies? If Bill kissed you, he was just being affectionate, because he loves you – not that you deserve his love.' She slapped me hard across the face. 'You're an evil, ungrateful liar.

I can't believe a word you say. Bill is a good man who has been nothing but kind to you, and this is how you repay him! Now there's no one left who loves you and it's all your own fault.'

I was thinking that if what he did was affection I didn't want it. It hurt. It scared me. I didn't want it to happen again. But I didn't dare say any of this to Mum as she stood in front of me, shouting at the top of her voice, going red in the face with the strength of her fury.

'Get up to your bedroom right now!' she finished. 'And I don't want to hear you ever mentioning this again. Do you hear me?'

I nodded and ran upstairs, distraught. Uncle Bill had been right when he said no one would believe me. No one could protect me. I was completely on my own.

When I saw Dad at breakfast the next morning I tried to catch his eye to see if he would at least sympathise but he wouldn't look at me. I don't think he believed me either. If he had believed me, he would have stopped Bill ever coming to the house again. I know he would, because although he could never show it, I think he wanted to love me, but wasn't allowed. So that's why he couldn't even look at me.

'Here comes the liar!' Mum sneered whenever I walked into a room over the next few weeks. She treated me as if I had committed a crime, and seemed to be punishing me for reasons I couldn't begin to understand. If she had been cold to me before, it was a whole lot worse now. She was either ignoring me completely or being scathing and mean and making me feel even more the outsider in the family.

Uncle Bill didn't come round for a while after that, so at least I was safe from his attentions. But Mum's hatred of me had deepened; there was no question that she loathed and despised me now. I was the black sheep of the family. I had ruined her life.

Chapter Four

Every day, or so it seemed, Mum reminded me of how I made her life a misery. How I told lies and made things up. How things would have been so different if only I hadn't been born. The only thing I wanted, the one thing I craved and yearned for, was her love and approval, but I never got it. Nothing I did was ever good enough. I clung to the hope that one day she would be kind to me, one day she would be proud of me, one day she would love me. But that day never came.

School provided a respite from the unhappiness at home. I was a quiet girl but I had lots of friends. Children usually accept people at face value, and because I needed these friends I always tried to please everyone so they would like me and include me in their games. I wasn't academically brilliant, but I tried very hard at all my subjects and enjoyed my time at school. When I did well at something, I hurried straight home to tell Mum my news, but it always fell on deaf ears. There was never any praise or enthusiasm.

Mum had always wanted one of her children to be musical, and as none of the others seemed interested this fell to me. I thought in my naïvety that if I were good at playing an instrument then she would love me. I spent hours and hours practising the violin, my mother's choice, passing many exams and being chosen to play for the Youth Orchestra. But still this wasn't enough. Mum never came to hear me play when we gave concerts unless there was a guest of honour she wanted to meet, in which case she would appear at the end of the performance carrying a huge bouquet of flowers. Heads would turn, because she was such a striking woman, a larger-than-life character. When the music had finished and the encores had been taken, Mum would send my little sister Anne up onto the stage to present the guest of honour with the flowers. Everyone applauded and remarked on how cute she was and how kind and generous my mother had been to make such a lovely gesture.

I wanted to tell them that she was just play-acting. She was pretending to be kind, pretending to be generous, but no one outside the family ever saw beyond the public face. She was far too good at it.

I took up singing lessons with a lovely teacher called Mrs Conti, who gave me loads of encouragement. She was a large, round Italian lady with olive skin and dark, almost black hair, who came to choir practice dressed in bright floral skirts and vivid blouses. She wore lots of jangly jewellery and I thought she was wonderful.

On one occasion I was chosen to sing 'Where'er you walk', a lovely Handel aria, at a concert in the Albert Hall, and we were told there would be television celebrities in the audience. I was very nervous at the prospect, but also very excited. Surely this would make Mum proud?

I rushed home to tell her the news. She was making the tea as I ran into the kitchen.

'I'm going to sing at the Albert Hall, sing on my own!' I just couldn't help myself.

'Will you stop that shouting,' she yelled at me. 'Just shut up that noise.'

'I'm going to sing at the Albert Hall,' I cried again. 'The Albert Hall, in London! In front of famous people.'

Hope was alive. She must be proud of me now.

She laughed harshly. 'So what's all the fuss about? If you think I'm going to waste my time going all that way to see people I can see on the TV in my own front room, then you're more stupid than I thought.'

We were the first people in our street to get a television and Mum was always referring to it. The neighbours would come at seven o'clock every evening and crowd round to watch the news, and Mum loved the kudos this gave her.

I spoke in a very small voice, trying hard not to cry: 'But I'm going to sing solo.'

I won't cry, I told myself. I won't.

'Well, I'm certainly not going to listen to that,' she said nastily. 'I wouldn't waste my time and effort.'

My bubble of excitement burst and disappointment flooded over me. I didn't want to sing in the Albert Hall now. There was no point. I went up to my room feeling very heavy and sad. Hope was dashed.

Next day I went to tell my singing teacher that I had changed my mind and she would have to find someone else to sing the solo.

This putting me down, this failure to praise my efforts was a regular occurrence in my young life. Once there was a writing competition at school and I wrote a story about Jack Frost. It was sprinkled with verse and my headmistress thought it was so good that she entered it into the county competition. It won the county prize and then it went up for the national competition and won that as well. It also won the overall prize for story content, style and poetry. My teachers were very proud. I wasn't sure what 'national' meant but it sounded important. Surely Mum would be proud of me now?

I rushed home with a copy of my story in my hand. 'Mum, I wrote a story about Jack Frost and my head teacher entered it for a competition and it won!' I tried not to show too much excitement, even though my tummy was letting me down. 'It won the local competition then another and then it won the bigger one, I think it was called the national competition.'

I waited for something. I'm not sure what, but I waited.

Did she hear me? Did she understand the hugeness of this happening?

I went on: 'They say it will be at the National Exhibition and will be on display for everyone to read and will be sent round all the schools in the area. Isn't that good?'

Why did I expect this to be different? Why did I think that this story success would have changed things?

'I don't know why you look so pleased with yourself,' Mum said. 'It's only a story and you probably copied it anyway. You're no good at anything. Start getting the table set for dinner and stop wasting my time.'

Maybe my life would have been easier if I had given up hope of ever pleasing her instead of constantly trying to achieve the impossible. But still I clung onto hope, no matter how futile. I couldn't stop hoping that one day, if I just won enough prizes and got good enough marks, surely she would have to love me the way she loved my sisters and brother? Mum always made a huge deal of any of their achievements. I wasn't jealous but just wished that one time she would show the same kind of interest in me.

But why would she? I was different, unlovable, unwanted. An unfortunate mistake.

As time went on, I became withdrawn and depressed at home. I was still traumatised by the attacks by Uncle Bill, the one person who I thought had loved me. I felt desperately upset when I thought about the nice memories of him being kind to me, back before his love changed into something horrible, into a kind of love I didn't want. Now no one loved me at all.

I continued to work hard at school and poured out my private thoughts in stories and poems, but I stopped bringing work home to show Mum because I knew she wasn't interested.

One day when I was about eight I wrote a very sad little story about a girl who felt unloved and unwanted. Because it was how I felt, I wrote it from the bottom of my heart. It caused a storm in my life, and if I had realised what the outcome was going to be I would never have written it.

The little girl in my story knew she wasn't wanted and knew her mother never loved her. I wrote that she was confused about why her brother and sisters were loved and treated well when she wasn't. I said she tried hard to please her mother but that her mother never seemed happy with anything she did. This made the little girl very sad and she felt very alone. Her mother referred to her as a mistake, but this little girl hoped that one day her mother would realise that she did love this child after all, and that hope kept her going. She would realise that there had been no mistake and then she would treat the little girl in the same way she treated her other children. And as in all make-believe, they lived happily ever after.

My teacher was very concerned about the content of the story and felt, I suppose, that only a child who had experienced great emotional pain could have written it. She was so concerned that she told me to ask my mother to come into school and discuss it with her.

Mum refused to come, saying she was far too busy.

The teacher must have been very worried indeed because the next day after school she turned up at our front door. I was sent to my room but I listened from the top of the stairs.

'I'm concerned about a story Cassie wrote in class,' my teacher said. 'I wonder if you would have a look at it and tell me what you think.'

'I haven't got time for this,' Mum said impatiently.

'If you don't mind, I think it's important.'

After some persuasion, Mum agreed to read the story and when she finished I heard the sound of her throwing the book down on the table.

'I wouldn't worry about this. She's got a vivid imagination. She's always making things up. She's a terrible liar. You wouldn't believe the stories she comes out with at home.'

The teacher persisted in wondering if anything was wrong but Mum was adamant that I was perfectly happy and the only thing I suffered from was an overactive imagination that made me make up lies.

As soon as the teacher had gone, Mum ordered me down-stairs and into the best room, a room that was usually kept for special occasions like Christmas.

But it wasn't Christmas.

'Do you feel like the child in this story?' she asked, holding out my English book. 'Is this how you really feel?'

At first I was afraid to confess that yes, I did feel like that, but then I was taken in by her play-acting and began to believe she was concerned. 'Well, yes, I do feel like that,' I said timidly. 'I do feel different and not wanted at home.' There was no reaction so I continued. 'All I ever wanted is for you to love me, but when I told you about what happened with Uncle Bill you didn't seem to care. You didn't even believe me. I don't under-stand why you didn't do something. He hurt me and scared me, and it was horrible.' My eyes welled up at the memory.

Suddenly, the woman in front of me erupted like a volcano. She grabbed my shoulders and shook me violently then slapped my face over and over, all the time screaming at me. 'You're the most ungrateful child ever to have been born. How can you say you're not loved? It was all lies about Bill. He would never hurt you and do those awful things. How could you write down all those dreadful things in that story and let your teacher see them?'

Mum glared down at me for a while, as if considering something. Suddenly she seemed to come to a decision: 'You'll have to go and live somewhere else. Yes, that's it. Perhaps in a children's home,' she grimaced. 'Then you would know what it's like not to be loved!'

That was the threat Uncle Bill had made, that I would be sent away to an awful place where bad things would happen to me. Why was Mum saying this? She had asked me how I felt. Should I have lied and said I made it all up, that it was just a story?

In the middle of all of this drama, Dad came home from work and wanted to know what was going on.

'Your little girl doesn't love us any more and she wants to leave home,' Mum told him, then began to cry with big, loud, choking sobs.

I tried to say that this wasn't true but Mum cried even louder, drowning me out, so I ran up to my room and hid under the bedclothes. My only place of safety.

Later that evening no one seemed to know where Mum was. She had done one of her disappearing acts, so Dad and I went out looking for her. It was cold, dark and wet and we seemed to be searching for hours. As a last resort I called in at the fish and chip shop owned by a neighbour, Auntie Mary, who was a friend of Mum's. I asked if she had seen Mum but she claimed she hadn't been by all day. While we were talking, I thought I caught a glimpse of Mum walking past the window that looked out from Auntie Mary's house into the back of the shop. I was sure I saw her, but Mary denied it.

Eventually we went home, but Auntie Mary came in to talk to Dad later. I listened from my usual spot at the top of the stairs.

'Your wife came to see me and she's desperately upset. She says your ungrateful daughter has been spreading ugly rumours about being ill-treated and unloved, and now she doesn't want to come home any more.'

I felt terrible. I had never *told* anyone how I felt. I'd only written about it in the story, and now I wished I'd never done that.

I rushed down the stairs and confronted Auntie Mary. 'Please tell Mum I didn't mean it. Tell her I love her and please tell her to come home.'

Mum let us sweat it out for a few more hours before she deigned to come back. As soon as I heard the door opening, I rushed down to apologise and tell her I hadn't meant it.

'Get away from me!' she screamed. 'Get away, you nasty child. You hurt me badly with all your lies and insinuations. I'm a good mother and you should be grateful to me. I do everything for you and this is how you repay me.' At this she fell into her chair and began to cry.

My brother and sisters crowded round to comfort her. Dad said nothing, just left the room to go to his safe place, the shed in the back garden. I cowered in the background, once more the outsider, the person no one loved or wanted.

After this episode things got much worse for me. Confident that she occupied the moral high ground, Mum decided that Uncle Bill could come back into our lives again. The day he came back, he was armed with flowers for Mum and presents for us children.

'Can I take Cassie out for a ride, Kath?' he asked, looking at me with the same funny expression he'd had when he hurt and scared me before. 'We won't be long. I've missed our trips out.'

I remember thinking that I hadn't missed him at all. I wanted to scream, 'No, you can't take me out.' But I didn't. It wouldn't have made any difference.

'Yes, of course you can,' my mother replied. 'She's not doing anything useful, so take as long as you like.'

I walked with him to the car, feet dragging, and climbed into the front seat feeling very nervous. We drove to a quiet side road and he stopped the car. This is OK, I thought, this is OK, nothing will happen here. But I was wrong.

Without saying a word, he reached over and put his hand up my skirt and into my panties then started rubbing his fingers up and down on my private parts and groaning.

I was terrified. What could I do? How could I stop him? There was no one around to hear me if I screamed. I couldn't jump out of the car and run away because I didn't know where we were.

'Please don't,' I whispered. 'Please stop.'

'You don't really want me to stop,' he said. 'I've got a new game we can play. Won't that be fun?'

I looked at his face, the face I used to think of as friendly, and I knew that whatever it was, I wasn't going to enjoy it.

'The game is for you to find the love toy. I've hidden it in my trousers and you have to find it. Come on! Here's what you do.' He took my hand and pulled it to the front of his trousers and rubbed it up and down.

I was scared and wanted it to stop. This wasn't a game I liked. My toys were fun. Games were something you were supposed to enjoy, not something nasty and horrible.

'Come on, Cassie. You know how much I love you.' He kissed my face, pushing my hand harder against him.

If that was what love meant, I didn't want it. I'd always thought love was gentle and kind and that you didn't hurt the person you loved, but Uncle Bill kept on hurting me.

Now he had unfastened his trousers and was pushing my hand inside where it felt all squelchy. He moved it up and down on his private part, his awfulness, and I felt it get bigger. I pulled my hand away and tried to hide it somewhere safe, like under my jumper, but he wouldn't let me do that. He was groaning and squirming around, making me hold tightly onto this nasty part of his body. Then I felt yucky whitish stuff all over my fingers, making me want to retch. It was horrible and sticky and I supposed it must be wee. Why would he do that to me? I was scared to death and he just didn't care.

He pulled a hankie from his pocket and cleaned himself up then he threw it onto my lap. 'Wipe your hands off and we'll go home,' he said in a cold voice.

I was yearning to be at home, in the relative safety of my bedroom, so I wiped my hands and sat still and silent as he drove me back then dropped me off outside our house.

I ran straight upstairs to the bathroom and let the water gush over my trembling hands. I couldn't make sense of it at all. I felt lonely and desperate. Was this how love was supposed to be? Was it meant to cause you pain and disgust till you felt sick to your stomach? There was no one I could ask. I felt too ashamed. My feelings were too intense, too heavy. I couldn't find peace anywhere. I had told my mother what he had done and she hadn't believed me, so now there was no one left who could help me.

Soon Uncle Bill wanted us to play his games at every opportunity he had, whenever he could get me on his own – all in the name of 'love'. I would beg Mum to tell him I couldn't go out with him.

'Please, Mum. Please. I don't want to go. Don't make me.'

'You ungrateful girl!' she'd snap. 'Bill goes to a lot of trouble to give you a nice time. He loves you – goodness knows why – so you can just jolly well go out with him when he can find the time for you and count yourself lucky.'

Lucky. That was one thing I never felt as a child. Sometimes I thought I must be the unluckiest child in the whole wide world.

Chapter Five

The in-between times, when I wasn't with Uncle Bill or Mum, became the only bits that kept me going. My singing was an in-between time, as was school, but the most important in-between time was the time I spent with Claire.

Claire was a skitty, funny, happy girl who was just lovely to be around. I often went to her house at weekends and during the holidays and I used to love the way her parents were with her. They laughed together and hugged each other and it all seemed so natural and easy. Claire's mum often invited me to stay overnight and I was able to truly relax then, knowing there were hours ahead of me in which no one would shout at me or pull my hair and hit me, and that there was no chance of Uncle Bill coming to take me out. Sometimes Mum banned me from staying over at Claire's because she didn't want me to enjoy myself, but most of the time she would let me because it got me out from under her feet.

The times I spent with Claire and her family allowed me to daydream. I wished I belonged there. I tried to pretend that they were my family, and that her mum and dad were mine too. I know her parents really cared about me because of the clothes they bought me and the trips they took me on as part of their family. Why couldn't I become one of them?

Claire and I liked playing games of make-believe. Once we made up a play called *Princess Tallulah and the Emperor's Treasure* and invited some of the other children in her street to act in it. I played Princess Tallulah, who was beautiful and kind, and I loved the feeling of being someone else, someone happy.

Sometimes we pretended we were grown-up ladies out for lunch with each other. We'd dress up smartly and go into the café in Littlewood's department store, Claire with her pocket money and me with any pennies I'd managed to save from doing odd jobs for neighbours. We'd order one bowl of 'Piping Hot Tomato Soup' and a roll to share. Sometimes I poured a little bit of vinegar into the soup, just because I could. It didn't improve the flavour, but Mum would never let me have vinegar at home because she said it soured the blood. So, on a Saturday in Littlewoods, I poured vinegar in my soup. It felt good to be able to do this without her watching and telling me off.

When we were nine, Claire and I joined the Girls' Life Brigade, where we worked to earn badges for things like handicraft, housekeeping and reading books. The Brigade meetings were every Friday night and I started going to Claire's after school on Friday then staying the night after the meeting. Her mum would make us baked beans on toast and we would watch *Popeye* together on television. There was never any pressure to eat foods I didn't like, such as green vegetables. We'd have a lovely girly time, giggling as we dropped off to sleep in the same room.

Sometimes I watched Claire and wondered if there was anyone like Uncle Bill who touched her and hurt her, but I couldn't imagine that there was. She was too clean and happy, untouched by anything nasty in the world. Occasionally I thought about telling her what Uncle Bill did. I'd rehearse the words over and over in my head. Maybe I should just hint at it and see how she reacted?

But if my own mum didn't believe me, why should anyone else? And the threat of being sent to a children's home was always hanging over me. I didn't know anyone who had been to one but everything I heard about them sounded grim. Our English teacher, Mrs Rutherford, once read us a story about a little girl who lived in a children's home and it sounded like an awful place to be. The teachers were cruel and locked the girl in a cupboard. The children were kept short of food and were beaten if they were naughty. I didn't want to go somewhere like that, so I couldn't risk telling.

Besides, what if Claire thought it was my fault? What if she told her mum and they decided I couldn't come to their house any more because I was tainted, or bad? I had been told so often at home that I was a bad person that there was part of me that believed whatever was happening was my own fault. I must deserve it when Bill put his hand inside my panties and rubbed till it felt raw, or made me hold his love toy while he made strange grunting noises. I didn't want to risk losing my make-believe family, who were so kind to me. That's why I couldn't tell Claire about these things that made me feel sick and terrified. I couldn't tell anyone.

It would never have occurred to me to tell a teacher at school, or a neighbour, or one of my two nans. They'd tell Mum and she would go berserk. My life wouldn't be worth living. It would be even worse than the drama after I wrote that story about a little girl who was unwanted and unloved. I would probably be sent straight to the children's home, and goodness knows what would happen there.

That only left Dad, but I knew he would never stand up to Mum. He was no match for her. She tormented him almost as much as she tormented me. She would constantly tell him that he was useless, and that he didn't know anything. When she was short of money, it would always be his fault: 'You don't earn enough to keep us. You make it hard for me to put food on the table, you good for nothing …' She would often tell him that the day she met him was the worst day of her life, and once she brought tears to his eyes by shouting that she should have gone when she had the chance. I had no idea what this meant – where could she have gone? – but Dad looked so sad that it stuck in my memory.

She'd set up situations just to make him look foolish, and that made me feel protective towards him. The last thing I'd want would be to get him into any more trouble by telling him my problems.

On my birthdays, we would be sitting round the table at teatime when Dad got in from work, wet and cold from riding his bike through the November chill. He was a slight man, probably a bit taller than Mum but much thinner. She'd be standing waiting for him, arms folded.

'Where's Cassie's present then?' she'd demand.

He'd look startled, having had no idea it was my birthday. Like most men, he wasn't good at remembering dates.

'Don't tell me you've forgotten the poor child's present again? Didn't you even get her a card?'

'I didn't know …' he'd stumble, sad and embarrassed.

I tried to tell him it was OK, I didn't mind, but Mum would continue to taunt him until he slunk off out the back door to the haven of his shed.

My brother and sisters always got great piles of presents on their birthdays but there would be nothing on mine, and Mum always blamed Dad for it. I can't remember what age I was when it eventually occurred to me that Mum was the one who bought the others' presents, because Dad was at work all day and had no time to get to the shops. Besides, it was Mum who held the purse strings in the household. The whole teatime scene when she blamed him was just a charade, designed to make both of us feel bad.

One year, as my birthday approached, I decided to do something about it so I earned some money running errands for a neighbour. On the day before my birthday, I bought some colouring pencils, a book and some wrapping paper and I wrapped them up as a present.

After tea, I went out to Dad's shed and put the little parcel into his hand.

'It's my birthday tomorrow,' I said quietly, 'and I know you don't have time to shop, so I bought these. They're just what I want.'

Now he wouldn't look bad in front of the family, and she wouldn't be able to have a go at him. There was a strange look in Dad's eyes: sad, but loving at the same time. I thought I would be sparing him from getting a row this year, but how wrong I was.

The next evening, when Dad came home from work, we were all sitting round the table as usual. Before Mum could say anything, he walked over and handed me the parcel.

'Happy birthday, Cassie. Hope you like these,' he said softly and we smiled a secret smile.

All eyes turned expectantly to Mum. Surely she would be pleased he had remembered? Instead, she went berserk and started shouting abuse at both of us.

'What do you think you're playing at, trying to make a fool out of me?' she yelled at Dad. Then she turned to me. 'You wicked, wicked girl. You put him up to this! How dare you!' She grabbed me by the arm, shaking me violently. 'Get out of my sight, I can't bear to look at you!'

I didn't dare to look at Dad as I turned and made my way upstairs without any tea. I could still hear her yelling at him as I closed my bedroom door and lay down on the bed. My plan for an argument-free birthday had backfired badly. It seemed that no matter how hard I tried to please her I was destined always to get things wrong. I kept hoping that one day she would be proud of me, one day she would realise she loved me, but that day never seemed to come.

Christmas was another time when Mum made it very clear that I was at the bottom of the pecking order in our family. Every year my brother and sisters and I wrote letters to Santa Claus and sent them up the chimney – 'Write whatever you want,' Mum would urge us – and every year my siblings would get what they had asked for and I would only get a couple of small, cheap toys. She had to get me something because both my nans would be there and they'd have asked questions if she didn't, but it was usually just sweets or cardboard cut-out dolls or a comic, while my siblings got big presents like bicycles and rollerskates.

One year, when I was nine or ten, I asked Santa for a bicycle. Tom, Ellen and Rosie all had bicycles and Anne was still too young for one at the age of four. As we came downstairs that Christmas morning, I peeked out the kitchen door and saw two large, bicycle-shaped presents all wrapped up in Christmas paper. One was bigger than the other. My heart leapt in excitement. I knew Tom had asked for a new bike, so the bigger one must be for him while the smaller one was for me. I thought of all the things I would do on my bike: cycling round to Claire's house, whizzing downhill with the wind in my hair. At last I was being given what I had asked for! Mum must care about me after all.

After breakfast, we went into the best room. I was so excited. We emptied our stockings first then Mum started bringing in the bigger presents. First of all she brought in the larger bicycle-shaped present and gave it to Tom. He leapt for joy and couldn't get the wrapping paper off fast enough. I was so happy for him, not only because I loved my brother, but also because I was anticipating my own joy in the following few minutes. Then it happened.

Mum spoke to my little sister: 'Watch the doorway, Anne. We have a very special present for you.'

My little sister stood up and watched as Dad brought in the second bicycle-shaped present. My heart lurched as he placed it next to her. It was a bike, a too-big-for-her bike. *My* bike.

I felt heavy, devastated, heartbroken. I looked at Mum and realised she was watching me with a strange smile on her face, enjoying my disappointment. I looked away again quickly, trying to pretend I hadn't seen, but that look stayed in my mind.

She had won again.

She really didn't love me.

Nana B, Dad's mum, reached out and gave me a quick hug, perhaps sensing my disappointment even though I tried not to let it show. My nans were lovely people but neither of them dared stand up to Mum, and that meant that they didn't dare be too openly affectionate to me in front of her.

There was another Christmas when Mum lifted my hopes only to dash them again. I had asked for a life-size baby doll that I'd seen for sale in town. I only had one doll, Suzie, but I loved her and spent a lot of time bathing, dressing and pretending to feed her. Then I fell in love with the life-size doll, a boy doll, as soon as I saw it.

One of my jobs around the house was to make Mum's bed, and the week before Christmas, as I moved her bedside table to tuck in the sheet, I spotted a box. A baby-doll-sized box. Of course I knew I shouldn't look. But I did. I was only a little girl doing grown-up chores, and I couldn't resist. As I lifted the lid, I could see the glowing china face and painted hair. Post-war, dolls had painted-on hair, not hair you could touch and comb like today's dolls. He was beautiful. I wanted to lift him out of the box and hold him in my arms. I wanted to make his eyes open to see if they were blue. I wanted them to be blue. Not that that would have mattered – they could have been any colour and I'd have loved him.

I was beside myself with excitement as Christmas approached. None of the others liked dolls. My sisters were far too old and Anne was a tomboy, more interested in outdoor games. The doll had to be for me. It couldn't be for anyone else.

Christmas morning finally came and we were all summoned to the 'best room'. Mum brought in a large parcel for my brother first and he opened it to find a metal racing car painted in bright colours. He was thrilled with it and I was happy for him.

Then in came my dad, carrying the box. Although it was wrapped in Christmas wrapping, I knew it held the china doll. I half-stood up, ready for him to hand it to me, and then I heard Mum's words and I froze.

'This is your main present,' she said to my little sister. 'Come and see what we've bought you. You'll love it.'

She glanced over at me, looking for my reaction, her eyes narrowed, as the box was placed on the floor in front of the

I did tell, I did

child who didn't like dolls. The child who hadn't asked for a doll.

My little sister opened the parcel and said a polite thank-you. I held my breath. Perhaps they had another baby doll. Perhaps they would bring mine in next. Perhaps … perhaps I'd got it wrong again. Perhaps I wasn't to get one. Perhaps I was right the first time.

After all the other presents had been handed out, and my sister had tossed the baby doll aside, my dad came in holding another present.

'This is for you, Cassie,' he said. 'I made it specially.'

I didn't dare look at Mum in case she spoiled the moment. I ran over to him and took the parcel in my arms.

'How dare you have a present for *her*!' Mum screamed. 'How dare you do this in secret, without my permission? I never said you could, did I?'

For the first time in my life, I ignored Mum's angry words. I took the gift Dad was handing me and unwrapped it to find a beautiful, hand-made pink cot. A doll's cot. A cot for Suzie. I'd asked for a cradle the Christmas before and hadn't got it. Dad must have remembered and decided to make me one out in his shed. I thought he'd been spending a lot of time out there, and on a couple of occasions when I'd gone out to visit him I'd been disappointed that he didn't let me in. This must be why! He'd been making me a cot. I loved it. I loved him. I stood up and thanked him, with tears in my eyes.

But before I could fetch Suzie to show her the new bed, Mum, who was outraged, lifted this beautiful cot, the cot my

Dad had spent evening after evening making. She lifted it high in the air without a thought for anyone, without even looking at it properly, and she threw it against the wall. It shattered into lots of pink splintery pieces. What was left in her hand, she hurled at me.

'Did you really think I would let you have a present that had been made in deceit? Did you really expect me to let you have a present that you hadn't asked for or deserved?' Her voice was full of hate. 'It's shoddy, and made of painted tomato boxes. It's shabby and cheap. And although you don't deserve anything better, you won't have it, I'll make sure of that!'

I stood rooted to the spot, looking at her, then looking at Dad, and feeling numb. Did she really just do that? Was I seeing things? Did what I thought just happened, happen? Yes, it did, she had.

I must have done something very bad to deserve this mother. What had I ever done to her? Why did she hate me so much?

I would have loved that cot. The cot that my dad had worked on for weeks. The cot he made to make things better for me. But now there was no cot. Now there were broken bits of pink painted wood all over the best room floor.

No one moved.

No one spoke.

The room was silent. All you could hear were my tiny shivery sobs.

So Christmases and birthdays were times I learned to dislike, to put up with, just to get through. They never got any better. They were the perfect chance for Mum to show me how much she disliked my very being there. How the rest of her children were loved and I wasn't.

To get me through the bad times, I made up a little story in my head. I'd imagine it at night when I lay in bed unable to sleep, embellishing it with extra details as I went along. The story went like this.

One day there was a knock at the door of our house, the house where I lived with a mother who hated me. She called out to me to answer it. On the doorstep stood a handsome man and a beautiful lady. They were dressed really well. I imagined their clothes in detail, right down to the shoes, and the lady's handbag.

'We're here because there's been a terrible mistake,' the man said. 'A mistake of the gravest concern.' His voice was gentle, well-spoken.

The woman continued, 'When we were very young, we had a baby. A baby girl. Because of our ages, we were forced to give her away. We had no choice. But now we have changed our minds and want her back. We've come to put the mistake right and take the little girl home with us.'

'What age are you?' the man asked. 'And what's your name?'

I answered their questions and they looked at each other. 'It's you, our beloved baby. We've missed you so much. Will you come home with us?'

I was loved. I was wanted. I would belong. They took me home and from then on I was the happiest child alive.

Chapter Six

When I was ten years old and at home in bed one day with Asian flu, Mum left me in the house on my own and went out with Ellen and Rosie. They didn't tell me where they were going but they locked the door behind them, so at least I didn't have to worry about Uncle Bill turning up.

When Mum got back, she came upstairs holding a little bundle of black fur.

'This is for you,' she said. 'A present.'

I didn't believe her. It had to be a trick. Why would Mum buy me a present? I looked more closely and saw that it was a tiny black puppy with its pink tongue hanging out. He was looking up at me trustingly.

I stretched out my hands. 'Can I hold him?'

Mum pulled him away. 'Not right now. You have to learn how to take care of him first.'

He was a black poodle puppy, a toy dog who would never grow very big, and Mum called him Bobby. He was the most adorable dog I'd ever seen and I was quickly smitten. But I soon realised that the only reason why Mum said Bobby was mine was because she wanted me to be responsible for walking him, feeding him, toilet-training him, and looking after any aspects of his care that constituted chores, so that she could enjoy the fun bits of pet ownership, such as sitting with him on her knee, stroking him and feeding him titbits when she felt like it. The 'ownership' was selective, depending on whether anything needed to be done at the time. He was most definitely my dog whenever a mess needed to be cleared up.

I didn't mind at all, though. I took him out for walks at every opportunity, sometimes wandering as far as the sea, which was about four miles away from our home. Once there, I'd throw sticks for him on the beach and he'd fetch them and bring them back to me, or he would go for a swim while I paddled in the waves. Sometimes, if I had the money, I would buy an ice-cream and we would share it. I would break off the bottom of the cone and offer it to him with a little ice-cream in it and he would gulp it down. Then, if I had any money left, we'd take the open-topped bus back home again. We'd sit right at the front and Bobby would stand on my lap letting the wind lift his floppy ears.

One of the ways I made money was by helping my brother Tom with his paper round. He wasn't very good at getting up in the morning and most days he would tell me that he was running a bit late, he'd just be a minute and could I run into the shop and start to mark up his papers for him? I fell for it every time. I would rush off and mark the papers with the addresses and I'd have everything ready by the time he finally strolled in.

When we went out to do the paper round together, he would remain seated on his bike, roll up each paper then instruct me to deliver it to the appropriate house. My little legs would take me off as ordered, with Bobby running by my side, and I'd deliver the paper, then run back for the next one and the next and so on. At the end of the week, my brother would collect ten and sixpence from the newsagent and he'd give me the sixpence. Just sixpence, but that was OK. I didn't mind because I loved Tom, although he was completely spoiled by Mum.

Bobby provided me with a perfect excuse to leave the house when Mum's nagging was getting too much for me: time for another walk. He was a loving, affectionate dog and I quickly grew to love him dearly. He was loyal to me, running to the door to greet me as soon as I got home from school and following me around the house as I did my chores. When I was sad, after Mum had been screaming abuse at me, or after a trip out somewhere with Uncle Bill, Bobby would look up at me with his big dark eyes and it was as if he knew, and was saying, 'Don't worry, I love you.'

Times with Bobby were in-between times, good times, but there were bad things going on as well. Nasty things. Uncle Bill started coming to pick me up from school in his car on the days when he wasn't working.

'Isn't that kind of him?' Mum would coo. 'Say thank you, Cassie.'

On the way home, he'd always find some excuse to make a detour, then he'd park in the bluebell woods and make me do disgusting, awful things in the back of the car. And there was a horrible new development in his games. One time, after I had found the 'love toy' in his trousers, he told me I had to lick the foul thing until it was clean. When I said I couldn't, he tried to push my head down into his lap and force it into my mouth. I started to sob hysterically, terrified that I would choke to death, and at last he stopped, muttering crossly that I would have to do it another time. The thought was petrifying to me. Did people really do these things? How did they breathe? How did they stop themselves from retching and throwing up?

I was always looking for excuses to get out of accepting a lift with Uncle Bill: too much homework, chores to be done at home, Girls' Brigade on Fridays and, of course, walking the dog. I found another refuge at the age of ten when Mum volunteered me to sing in the local church choir. The choir had a dwindling population and needed some new voices. Trying to impress the vicar, Mum offered him my services and so it was arranged that I would have to sing at church twice on Sundays, attend a choir practice on Wednesday evenings, and then I'd have to be there some Saturdays for weddings as well. I was over the moon at this! Four times a week when Bill couldn't take me out and force me to do the things I hated with a passion. Four times a week when Mum couldn't yell at me or order me around. The choir was a refuge where I could be me, rather than the object of her anger and ridicule. I'd felt sure I'd be safe there. Safe from the evil that was Bill.

I had always enjoyed Sunday school back when I was younger, and I believed in the teachings of the church. Perhaps once I joined the choir, God would answer my prayers and keep me safe from now on. Perhaps God would protect me from Uncle Bill. That's what I wished more than anything else in the world.

I loved every aspect of being a member of the choir. The music was beautiful, the other singers were all very nice to me, and I liked the whole atmosphere of the church. I hadn't been singing there for long when our vicar, a lovely man who had been a missionary in Africa, asked if I wanted start confirmation classes so I could become a full member of the church. I said yes straight away, hoping that if I became a proper member of God's family I would be protected. Hoping that these classes would provide at least one more night a week when I was safe from unwelcome attention.

There was no one else to protect me. I'd told Mum what he did with me, that he touched me between the legs and hurt me, and still she waved me off gaily when he came to pick me up.

'Go on, my love,' she'd say. 'Have a nice time.' She never spoke harshly to me in front of Bill. She was all smiles and sweetness and light around him, but I knew that it was more than my life was worth to argue back. I'd tried that when I was seven and my life wasn't worth living for months afterwards.

And if I ever tried to resist Uncle Bill and stop him doing what he wanted, he would say that he had the right to do it, which puzzled me a lot. What gave him that right? Did all men have a right to make little girls hold their 'love toys'? Did all men have the right to touch them inside their panties?

'You know you like it,' he'd say. 'I can tell you do. Men know these things.'

But he was wrong. I hated it more than anything else in the world. It was the worst thing that ever happened to me, and it kept happening week in, week out, all year round. All I could think of was to keep myself as busy as I possibly could so that there was less time when I could be with him.

My eleventh birthday came and went and it was time to sit the Eleven Plus exams that would decide whether I was bright enough to go to the local grammar school or whether I had to attend the secondary modern. My mother was determined that I had to go to the grammar, not because she cared about my future prospects but because she wanted to be able to boast about it to the neighbours. Having a clever child would reflect well on her. Tom had failed the Eleven Plus because he never worked very hard at school but Mum couldn't stay angry with her precious boy for long. The pressure transferred to me. I had to be the one who was an academic success.

My grades at school had been slipping, though, with all the trauma and insecurity of my life. I hardly ever felt safe. I found it hard to trust anyone. I tried to study for the exams but my thoughts were elsewhere, constantly worrying every time there was a knock on the door that it would be Bill coming to pick me up and take me out for a drive, or that Mum would find some reason to pick on me for a household chore I hadn't done to her satisfaction.

I sat the first part of the exams, but before the second part came along I caught a cold and became very run-down. I couldn't seem to shake off a bad cough and sore throat, I was having trouble getting to sleep at night and I didn't have any appetite for food. On the day of the second part of the exams I struggled in to school and sat at my desk staring at the exam paper, feeling more and more weak and dizzy. Then I began a coughing fit and couldn't stop. One of the teachers came over to help me out of the room for a drink of water, and as I stood up the world went black and I collapsed on the floor of the exam hall.

I was taken home by my worried form teacher and a doctor was called, who listened to my chest and told me I had pneumonia. I'd have to take antibiotics and stay in bed for several weeks to get my strength back. If it got any worse, he said, I'd have to be admitted to hospital.

Mum was furious when she heard the news. She managed to act the concerned mother for as long as the doctor was there but as soon as he left she screamed at me: 'Typical! How am I supposed to look after you? As if I'm not busy enough.'

And then another thought occurred to her. 'I suppose this means you'll fail the Eleven Plus and you won't get in to the grammar school. You've done this deliberately to hurt me, haven't you? You're such a selfish child.'

I didn't see how catching pneumonia could possibly be my own fault. Being stuck at home for weeks on end with Mum looking after me was a horrific thought and not something I would ever have chosen deliberately. I wouldn't be able to escape by walking the dog or going to choir practice or confirmation classes. I would be at the mercy of her tongue-lashing all day, every day, and I felt far too weak to deal with it. I kept having hacking coughing fits that left me drained and exhausted. Everything was an effort, even breathing.

Then, when I thought things couldn't get any worse, Uncle Bill came round to visit. 'You need a bit of time off, Kath,' he said to Mum. 'You're a saint for looking after her like this, but if you want to nip out to the shops or to get your hair done, I don't mind sitting with her. In fact, it would be a pleasure.' He winked at me.

'No, Mum, don't go!' I protested weakly.

'Bless her, she wants her mum.' She smiled at Bill and raised her eyebrows. 'Don't be silly, dear. Your uncle is perfectly capable of looking after you. You'll be just fine.' And off she went with a clip-clop of her high heels down the path.

Bill sat on the edge of the bed, his eyes glittering, and he felt my forehead, which was burning with fever. 'Now we can have some fun,' he grinned. 'I've missed my little Cassie.'

I tried to jerk away as his hands dived under the covers, pulling up my nightdress, but there was no escape. He tried to climb on top of me but I began to wheeze and cough.

'Please don't,' I rasped. 'I can't breathe.'

I thought this would stop him and was relieved when he got off me.

'OK,' he said, 'we'll have to try something else.' He was very red in the face and seemed to be in a hurry. He opened his trousers then pulled me off the bed and tried to get me to kneel in front of him, but I couldn't balance.

'For goodness sake, just stand up and take this into your mouth.'

Not that again. Please, God, no. 'I can't,' I moaned desperately, shaking my head from side to side. 'Please, I can't.'

But he forced my mouth open and pushed inside, making me gag. I couldn't breathe because my nose was blocked with the cold. I thought my mouth was going to rip at the sides, he was so big. I kept gagging and gagging but still he wouldn't stop, and the coughing was trapped in my chest so I felt as though I was choking. The back of my neck hurt where his hand was gripping me. It was horrible, disgusting, nasty, awful.

As soon as he took it out of my mouth, I was sick all over the bedcovers.

'Oh, for God's sake,' he spat. 'I suppose you expect me to clear that up. Well, you can finish what you started first of all.'

He forced my hands around his 'love toy' and made me move them up and down until the white stuff squirted out, as it always did. I was completely at his mercy. There was nothing I could do. I lay helpless on my pillow, gasping for breath, too weak even to try and push him away.

'There! Wasn't that nice?' he commented after it was all over, and I looked at him aghast. Did he genuinely believe it was nice for me? How could he? It made me sick to my stomach. How was that nice?

From then on, during all the weeks I was ill, Bill came round regularly 'to let Mum have a bit of time to herself for a change'. That's what he said. But really, he came round so he could do whatever he wanted with me, while I was captive in my own bed in the middle of the working day, with nowhere to hide, nowhere to run.

In front of the rest of the family he would shower me with affection, bringing little presents such as my favourite sweetie cigarettes, but now I never ate them. They disgusted me because 'he' had touched them. In front of the others he would tell me how brave I was being, but as soon as we were alone he did exactly as he wanted, no matter how ill I was feeling. I would pray that he wouldn't come, asking God over and over again to protect me from this despicable, nasty man. Sometimes I would pretend to Mum that I felt better and would be OK on my own, or I'd beg her to stay at home with me instead of letting Bill look after me. But none of it worked. Life was very hard and I was desperately unhappy and scared all the time.

It was a huge relief when the doctor pronounced me fit again and I could get back to school, back to choir and confirmation classes, and back to keeping myself as busy as possible so I didn't have any time left over to spend with Uncle Bill. So I wasn't a complete prisoner of that evil, nasty man.

Chapter Seven

My confirmation classes were to be held on Tuesday nights in the vicarage, and I looked forward to them – but there was just one problem. When the class was over, all the other students were met by their parents and taken home, but my dad worked as a scout leader on Tuesdays so he couldn't meet me and there was no way my mum was going to leave the house in the cold to fetch me. Eventually it was agreed that I would walk home on my own.

However, when the vicar realised this, he wasn't happy. The nights were still dark and frosty, I was only eleven years old and I'd just recovered from pneumonia, so he insisted that he would walk me home himself. At least then I wouldn't be on my own and he could make sure I was wrapped up warmly. When we arrived at my house the first time, Uncle Bill was just leaving. The vicar said good evening and explained why he had escorted me home.

'That's very kind of you, vicar,' Bill said, 'but I can pick her up from now on. I always visit the family on Tuesdays so it wouldn't be a problem. Cassie will be safe with me.'

I felt panic rise in my tummy. I looked at Mum, willing her to say no, that wouldn't be necessary. But seeing a solution that would not involve any effort on her part, my mother agreed that Bill should start picking me up every Tuesday. It was an ideal solution, she said.

On the next Tuesday, although terrified, I got into Bill's car and to my surprise he drove me straight home. He came in for a coffee with Mum afterwards, and all seemed well. I was so relieved that I tried hard to convince myself that everything would be all right now. I hoped that from now on he would leave me alone. Hope was my byword.

The next Tuesday evening I climbed into his car feeling a little more confident. He told me he had to get some petrol on the way home and so he drove off in the opposite direction, to a garage. He asked me how the class had been and, after filling the car, he set off again in the dark. I didn't have a good sense of direction and it was some time before I realised that we weren't going in the direction of home.

'Where are we?' I asked, timidly.

Bill didn't answer me, but seconds later he drove off the road into a field. It was pitch black outside and I began to feel very scared. I slid as far over on the seat as I could and huddled against the door.

'You are the most important person in my life and you mean the world to me,' Bill said as he inched closer. At that time, cars didn't have separate seats in the front. It was one long seat made of leather, which was easy to slide on, and there was no handbrake and gear stick in the middle, as there would be in a modern car.

My heart was pounding, but I was so terrified I couldn't speak.

'I love you so much. You know that, don't you?'

I didn't want him to love me. Not now that I knew what it meant.

'I just want to show you how much I love you,' he said, grabbing hold of me and covering my face with his slobbery kisses. I remember he smelled of whisky, a smell that I would hate for the rest of my life. Mum often gave him a glass when he came to the house.

I found my tongue at last. 'I want to go home. They'll worry if I'm late.' But as I spoke, I knew that of course they wouldn't. Mum wouldn't worry because she knew I was with him and, according to her, he loved me.

Uncle Bill took no notice. He was hot and sweaty, a film of moisture on his skin. He pulled me down so that I was lying on the hard leather and started tearing at my underclothes.

I tried to scream but nothing came out of my mouth. There was no one to hear out there in the field anyway.

Then he grabbed my hand and made me touch his body. 'Come on, you know you like it. Make me feel good. Come on.' His voice was husky and urgent.

He pulled open his trousers and lay on top of me and I felt the awfulness of his 'love toy' twitching against me. I was utterly repulsed.

In panic, I began to struggle as hard as I could but I was trapped underneath his weight. 'Please, please take me home. I want to go home,' I sobbed, but he wasn't listening.

He was breathing heavily now, fumbling between my legs, prodding and hurting me, oblivious to my tears.

And then I suddenly felt a new pain, a hot, terrible, tearing pain between my legs. It was as if I was being torn in half. I couldn't work out what had happened but Uncle Bill was bouncing on me now, groaning in his throat, pounding away between my legs, and I felt as though he was somehow inside me.

Now I couldn't cry out. The pain was so terrifying, I thought it was going to kill me. I'd never felt anything like it before and I actually wanted to die rather than go on like this. It went on and on until finally my uncle gave one last groan and slumped on top of me, squashing my face in his armpit.

I lay, my neck twisted to one side, feeling the horrible sharp pain between my legs. I had no idea what had just happened to me. Was this what grown-ups did? Is that what love was about?

Uncle Bill pushed himself up and started buttoning his trousers. I couldn't bear to look at him. I was shattered, physically and emotionally. My tummy and 'private bits' were burning and hurting badly. This couldn't be love, or anything like it. If it was, I didn't ever want to be loved. I had been taught at church that it was wrong to hate, but I felt hatred for the man in the car beside me who was combing his hair in the mirror and humming under his breath.

He started the car and began to drive home, still humming and obviously very pleased about this new development. I tidied myself up as if in a hypnotic trance, then turned to stare out the window at the dark shapes outside. I saw houses with their lights on, looking cosy and inviting, and I wished I lived in any of them. Anywhere but the place I really lived, where there was a mother who didn't care about me, who let me go out with this evil man.

When we reached the house, my uncle turned and looked at me, his little victim, and smiled a smile that I would learn to hate and fear over the next few months and years.

'You can't tell anyone what happened,' he told me, 'because you know no one will believe you.' He patted my knee. 'Your mum is a good friend of mine. She didn't believe you when you told her before and she won't now. Besides, you know how upset she was and what happened afterwards ...' He paused to let the threat sink in, smug in the knowledge that Mum wouldn't listen to a word against him. 'Let's just keep it our little secret, Cassie. OK? Off you go. Night, night.'

As I got out of the car I saw Mum at the window and Uncle Bill waved cheerily to her before driving away. I went indoors and called out in a shaky voice that I was tired, then I ran upstairs to the bathroom. I locked the door and finally all my strength left me and I collapsed on the floor, my whole body shaking.

After a while, I ran some water in the bath and started to take my clothes off. It still hurt very badly between my legs and when I pulled my panties down I was horrified to see blood on them. What on earth had happened to me? All I wanted to do was cleanse my body of this horrible experience as soon as possible. I scrubbed and scrubbed at my bruised flesh, all the while sobbing silently. What had I ever done to deserve this? Why was I being punished? Why wouldn't God save me?

After washing myself thoroughly and scrubbing the blood out of my panties, I scurried to my room and went to bed. I huddled under the blankets and tried to sleep, but my thoughts were racing. Every time I closed my eyes I felt his hot smelly breath on my face and his sweaty body against mine. I wanted to scream out loud but I couldn't. I wanted to run to someone to be held, but I couldn't. I began to cry with huge racking sobs, but that made me feel even more isolated. I shared a room with Ellen and Rosie at the time, but they were both out. Ellen had a boyfriend and Rosie worked late during the week. I couldn't have told them, anyway. I couldn't have told anyone because no one would believe me.

My dog Bobby came and licked my hand, trying to comfort me, and I lifted him up onto the bed for a cuddle. I prayed that sleep would come so that I would no longer have those horrible images in my head. I prayed that when I awoke I would find it had all been a bad dream. Finally I nodded off out of sheer exhaustion.

When I opened my eyes next morning, I knew straight away it hadn't been a dream. The pain in my tummy seemed worse than the night before and I had a throbbing feeling between my legs in the part where he had hurt me.

Dad looked round the bedroom door. 'Time for school, Cassie,' he said.

'I don't feel well,' I mumbled.

He came over to look down at me and for a moment I froze, thinking 'Oh no! Not him too.' I knew in my heart that my beloved dad would never hurt me, but a great deal of damage had been done the evening before. My trust had been betrayed and, now that I knew what men were capable of, for a moment I didn't even trust him.

'You don't look too well,' he said kindly. 'Perhaps you're coming down with a bug. Just lie there and I'll tell your mum that you're staying in bed today.' He tucked the blanket gently round me then headed off downstairs.

The sound of my parents rowing did nothing to comfort me. It was the last thing I needed and, once again, I hid under the bedclothes, trying to blot out the world. I heard my mother pound up the stairs and thunder into my bedroom.

'Get up for school!' she demanded. 'You know I'm supposed to go out with my friends today and you're just being selfish and trying to spoil things for me. Don't think I am going to put this off to look after you!' She glared at me. 'There's nothing wrong with you anyway. I'm not taken in as easily as your dad.'

Then she looked at me more closely. 'Hmm … Maybe you do look a bit peaky.' Was she suddenly going to have a burst of maternal concern? Suddenly going to put her arms round me and reassure me that she would look after me? No, of course not. She was furious. 'That's typical! I suppose I'll have to put off my day out now!'

More than at any other time in my life, I yearned for her to be a mother to me that morning. I was desperate for comfort. Couldn't she see how devastated I was? Didn't she have any natural maternal instincts towards me at all? But it seemed she didn't.

'I'll be OK on my own,' I told her quietly. 'I'll stay in bed for most of the day. I'm sure I'll feel better soon.'

The relief on her face was obvious. I didn't show her how much this upset me. Make-believe time again.

I tried to imagine what a real mother, like Claire's mother, would do if their daughter was lying in bed, distraught and in pain. Surely they would sense that they were hurting and try to comfort them? Claire's mum always asked her how she was, listened carefully to the answers and went to great pains to reassure her if she was upset about anything. But then I couldn't believe that Claire's mum would let a man like Uncle Bill anywhere near her daughter. She would have believed Claire if she told her what that man had done, way back in the beginning. She would never have let Claire go through the horrific experiences I'd been subjected to.

But Mum didn't see my pain, or didn't want to see it, and she went out to meet her friends as planned. I locked the doors and ran a bath. I was only eleven years old and all I knew was that the brutal events of the night before had left me feeling soiled and dirty. The bleeding had almost stopped but I was swollen and bruised down there. I lay in the warm bathwater and closed my eyes, wishing that I could keep them closed for a long, long time and that, on opening them, I would find that all the pain and fear had gone, and nothing would hurt me ever again.

How could I prevent this from happening? How could I avoid being taken home by this evil man who professed to love me but caused me so much pain and fear? If I stopped going to confirmation classes the vicar would want to know why, and if my mother hadn't believed me the first time, no one else would, I was sure. All day I tried to think of a way out of this awful trap. I prayed and prayed to the God who is supposed to keep you safe, just as I'd prayed before. But he wasn't listening, was he?

At four o'clock a friend called Wendy came to the house to see why I hadn't been to school. I said I had a tummy upset but would be back the next day, even though at that stage I couldn't imagine ever going out of the house again.

'But it's half-term,' she reminded me. 'School has broken up for the rest of the week.'

I had completely forgotten.

As we sat talking, I looked at her and wondered if she noticed anything different about me. I felt completely different to the way I had felt just twenty-four hours earlier. Something fundamental had changed and I didn't think I would ever be the same again.

But Wendy seemed to believe my tummy-ache lie and didn't notice anything else. She chatted away as normal about what had happened at school and passed on news of our other friends.

I was relieved it was half-term. Normally I loved school but I couldn't face going back to mix with my friends again the way

I was feeling. I was broken, damaged, dirty. Keeping up pretence was normal for me, but I wasn't sure I'd be able to pretend this time.

Before Wendy left, she asked if I would like to go on the Sunday school outing that Saturday, if I felt better. I said that I would. Anything rather than stay there, where he could get me if he chose to. It was agreed that I would spend the Friday night at her house, because it was to involve an early start in the morning.

The next few days were difficult. I was still very shaken. My body was hurting and the mental anguish was almost unbearable. What had he done to me? How could I stop him doing it again?

The Sunday school outing was light relief, though. All the teachers knew me and had heard that I hadn't been well. They could probably see that things weren't right with me and because of this gave me more attention and kindness than usual. This helped me a little and I began to feel slightly better.

I was still terrified about what would happen the following Tuesday. The thought of Bill, my abuser, picking me up and doing the same thing again made me feel physically sick. Wendy also attended confirmation classes, though, and this gave me an idea. I asked Mum if she could stay over at our house on a Tuesday night, and because Mum couldn't think of a reason why not, she agreed.

I was relieved beyond words when Wendy said she would love to do this, that it would be fun. It was as though a heavy horrible weight had been lifted from my shoulders. I was safe. God was listening after all.

When Uncle Bill turned up and realised he had two girls to ferry home on Tuesday, he seemed cross, but he could hardly retract the promise he'd made in front of the vicar and say he wasn't going to collect us after all. He could do nothing but let us into the back of the car and drive us straight home.

Soon it was spring and the evenings became light enough for us to walk home, and then the classes finished and I was confirmed. Wendy and I were very excited about the confirmation service. We were to wear white for this special occasion and I knew that white was a pure, special colour: brides wore white and so did angels. Wendy's mum was getting her a new dress and I asked if I could have one too. Mum said no, absolutely not, but Nana C volunteered to make me one. She was good at dressmaking and she created a beautiful white dress that made me feel as if I were a bride for the day.

Mum didn't attend my confirmation but my dad and Nana C did. Dad looked so proud of me that it made me wish Mum had been there, because I wished I could have seen that look on her face. But it wouldn't have been there; I knew that deep down.

During the service I prayed that I could be cleansed of the horrendous happenings of the past years. I prayed with all my heart that now I was a full member of the church, God would look after me. That at last he would start to listen to me. Surely he would.

Chapter Eight

Mum was furious when she got a letter home to say that I had failed the second part of the Eleven Plus because of collapsing in the middle of the exam. She charged up to the school for a crisis meeting with my teacher, cross that I was going to be sent to the secondary modern rather than the grammar school. She had never taken an interest in my education up to this point and had always failed to turn up for any meetings at school to discuss my progress, but now, all of a sudden, she seemed to feel that the school I went to next would reflect on her. She wanted the status of having a daughter who was bright enough for grammar school, and she wasn't giving in on that point.

'The stupid girl could at least have finished the exam paper,' she complained. 'Then at least she'd have stood a chance.'

'It wasn't her fault,' the teacher reasoned. 'She was ill on the day. It's just one of those things.'

'I don't care about that. She's failed me and she's failed the whole family. How could she?' Mum shouted, while I cowered behind her, mortified.

The teacher raised her eyebrows. 'Cassie has always done very well at school. She's a hard worker. Since you feel so strongly about this, I'll have a word with the headmistress and we'll see what can be done.'

I did well at school because it was my respite from home. School was where I felt normal, felt I belonged. I could engross myself in my lessons and blot out thoughts about the nasty events in the rest of my life. I strove to do my best and win praise from my teachers. Of course, what I really wanted was praise from Mum, but that wasn't going to happen. I never asked for much out of life and so wasn't disappointed when I didn't get much. But now I had failed her. Now I would never win her approval.

When Mum saw the headmistress, she explained that it was possible to re-sit the Eleven Plus and that she would be happy to enter me for the re-sit if that was what I wanted to do. This was at the end of the school year and in the September I would have to start at the local secondary modern, but I could take the re-sit in November and transfer to the grammar later on if I passed. She assured Mum that I had every chance of doing well, but added that it was up to me and that she and my form teacher would discuss it with me and ask what I preferred to do when the time came.

My mother left the meeting very angry and upset. She had never let me decide anything for myself before and didn't see why she should start now, as she told me in no uncertain terms that evening.

In the autumn term I started at the secondary modern, along with Claire and all my friends, and straight away I liked it there. The teachers were nice, the subjects we were taught were interesting and it had a good atmosphere about it. Then one evening I heard my parents talking. The school had been in touch with Mum to say it was time for me to make my decision about re-sitting the Eleven Plus. I heard her moaning to Dad about the fact that the teachers thought I should make the decision myself. She'd made up her mind I should go to the grammar, whether it was the best school for me or not, and that was that.

The following day the headmistress summoned my teacher and me into her office. The suggestion of a re-sit was discussed and I was asked what I wanted to do.

I asked if I could think about it and, because there was a deadline for applications for the exam, I was told I had to make my decision by the end of the week.

That evening I decided to try and talk to Mum and Dad about it. I really didn't want to move schools, because I felt safe where I was, where Claire and all my friends were. I didn't want to go to a big new school full of strangers with high academic standards and high pressure to go with it. But if it would make Mum happy, I thought maybe I should go along with her wishes. Maybe she would at last be pleased with me.

Just after I got home from school, I was on my way up to my room when I heard Mum and Dad arguing and my name being mentioned, so I stopped in the hall to listen.

'She should be grateful that she's in school at all,' Mum was screaming. 'Ever since she was born she's caused trouble. She's brought me nothing but pain and unhappiness.'

I couldn't begin to understand what she meant. What had I ever done to upset her so much? I hadn't played truant, as Tom often did, or stolen sweets from the local shop, or broken windows. Tom was always up to mischief, yet Mum just laughed off his pranks and stood up for him. But I'd never put a foot wrong. I was always too scared of her to break the rules or do anything remotely naughty.

Dad was trying to point out my achievements and telling her she should be proud of me, but she laughed harshly at that.

'How can I ever be proud of her after all she has done to me?' she shouted.

I was so confused, I wanted to rush in and ask what they were talking about, but a part of me was too afraid of finding out the answer. I knew she felt differently about me from the way she felt about the others, but I couldn't imagine why. I just felt that I must be bad inside to make her feel this way.

Mum was becoming hysterical with rage, but still Dad persevered. 'I think they're right to let Cassie decide whether she retakes the exam or not. She seems to be doing well at the secondary modern, and if she wants to stay maybe we should let her.'

Mum yelled, 'At least if she had a good education she could get a good job and start to repay me for her keep.'

That was confusing. Should I be paying Mum for my keep? Didn't parents usually pay to bring up their own children?

Before overhearing this row I had been ready to say that I would re-sit the exam and try to get into the grammar. Although I didn't want to leave my school, I had thought it might be an opportunity to make Mum proud of me. But now I knew this wasn't going to happen. No matter what I did, this woman would never be proud of me. At that moment I changed my mind. If I couldn't please her anyway, I might as well please myself. I was happy at the school I was in. The teachers liked me and my friends liked me. I was doing OK. If I got into the grammar I would lose all of this and still not gain the one thing I wanted – my mother's pride and love.

I decided to tell my parents my decision first thing the following morning, then I could escape to school straight after dropping the bombshell.

The next morning, after disturbed sleep, my courage was waning. I came down to breakfast feeling very nervous and I was relieved to see Dad still at the breakfast table. Perhaps he would support me in my decision.

'Have you thought about what your teachers asked you?' he questioned me.

'I've decided I would rather stay where I am,' I said nervously. 'You do understand my reasons, don't you?'

Before he could answer, Mum started to scream at me. 'It has nothing at all to do with him.'

I frowned. 'Why not? He *is* my dad.'

Mum slapped me round the face, harder than she'd ever slapped me before. I fell to the floor with the force of the blow and lay there, too stunned to cry. Mum leaned over me and began slapping me over and over again where I lay, with a ferocity that terrified me.

Dad pushed in front of her to protect me. 'That's enough now, leave her alone,' he said firmly.

Mum shouted, 'I will do what I want to her. I have every right to do as I please. Get out of the way. You have no rights as far as she is concerned!'

What on earth did she mean? I didn't understand the implications of what was being said. I only knew that once again I was in the wrong, for reasons I couldn't begin to understand, and I sensed that there was some kind of grown-up argument between Mum and Dad that I wasn't party to. Why did Mum have rights over me while Dad didn't? It made no sense at all.

As soon as I could escape, I ran upstairs to the bathroom and bathed my stinging face in cool water, then I tidied myself up and hurried off to school. Tom and Anne had left already and I didn't want to be late.

That morning I told my teacher that I had decided to stay at the secondary modern and she agreed that it was for the best. At least I wouldn't have to go through the trauma of changing school and making a whole new set of friends.

I was very wary of going home that afternoon but realised that if I were late it would give my mother yet another reason to be angry.

I walked into the kitchen and said hello to Mum and my sister Ellen, who was sitting chatting to her, but neither of them so much as acknowledged my presence. My heart sank. Mum could keep up these silences for weeks, and when she wasn't talking to me none of my siblings would speak to me either. To be fair to them, Mum was a force to be reckoned with, and if they had dared to talk to me they would find themselves on her bad side as well – a fate they didn't want to risk. But it meant I was totally isolated in the house. Dad retreated out to his shed after tea every evening, and I got the cold shoulder from everyone else right the way through to bedtime.

The deadline for re-sitting the examination came and went and still no one was speaking to me, but then Mum became ill with anaemia. She had to lie on the sofa all day long, and when I wasn't at school I was expected to wait on her hand and foot, making endless hot drinks, checking that she was comfortable, reading to her and generally caring for her. She was supposed to eat raw liver, and the job of chopping it into little pieces and feeding it to her with a fork fell to me.

'It makes me feel squeamish,' she claimed. 'If you feed it to me, at least I don't have to look at it.'

It used to make me feel ill too, but I'd do it to try and help her get well again. I never got any thanks, though.

Visitors remarked on how caring I was –'What a little angel,' one friend said – but to my mother I was just someone to order about until I fell into bed each night exhausted. No matter how hard I tried, I could do nothing right. It was a huge relief when she eventually recovered and things got back to normal in the house. My choice of school was never mentioned again and Mum never once enquired how I was getting on. She really didn't care now that I had failed her by not getting into the grammar.

And then, in the middle of the school year, I became ill again. I think I hadn't ever recovered fully from the pneumonia and I was still very weak. I was constantly tired, with aching joints, sores in my mouth, and I felt sick most of the time. At first the doctors weren't sure what was wrong with me. They thought I was anaemic, as Mum had been, and treated me with iron supplements, but that didn't seem to help. Nana C told me I had 'growing pains'. I spent a lot of time on the bed settee downstairs, so that whoever was looking after me didn't have to keep coming up the stairs with my meals and drinks. Uncle Bill had been round to visit but so far I hadn't been left on my own with him, which was a huge relief.

For a long time I had wanted to tell somebody about my ordeal at his hands, but who could I tell?

One day, after hearing that I was ill, the vicar of our church came round to visit me, and as this very kind holy man sat by my bedside chatting I seriously considered confiding in him. If I told a vicar, it would almost be like telling God. He'd have to do something to help, wouldn't he?

But then the doubts crept in. I'd told Mum and she hadn't believed me, had she? What if the vicar didn't believe me? He might think I was a liar who just wanted to hurt my Uncle Bill, the man who'd been kind enough to pick me up from confirmation classes and drive me home. I didn't want the vicar to think badly of me, so in the end I decided against confessing. It seemed too much of a risk to take.

While I was ill Mum didn't change the pattern of her life at all. If she had to go out, or wanted to go out, either Auntie

Mary who owned the fish and chip shop came in to look after me, or I was left on my own.

One afternoon while Auntie Mary was there, Uncle Bill came round. 'I thought I'd come and cheer you up,' he said.

I stared at him. Cheer me up? What did that mean? I didn't want his kind of cheering up. But at least I thought I would be safe because Auntie Mary was there. And then I heard the awful words.

'I don't mind looking after Cassie until her mum comes home,' Uncle Bill said, smiling.

I was terrified. I didn't know what to say to stop this from happening. Everyone thought they knew how much he loved me. Everyone thought they knew how kind he was to me. In fact, they knew nothing at all about what went on between us. No one knew.

Auntie Mary said, 'Well, I do have some shopping to do, and if you're sure, I'll leave you to look after her.' She left, happy that I was in safe hands. I was once again at the mercy of my abuser.

At first he sat by the side of the bed settee, reading a newspaper. I thought that if I pretended to sleep, he would go into the kitchen and leave me to rest. I closed my eyes and prayed that my deception would work. But God wasn't listening.

Suddenly I felt the blankets being pulled back. I kept my eyes closed tightly, as if the tighter I held on, the safer I would be. Then I felt my nightie being tugged. I held on to it even more tightly. I was cold with fear. I simply didn't know what to do. If I screamed, he would know I was awake, and then it would happen. Surely if I kept my eyes closed and held on to my nightie then it wouldn't happen?

His huge hands were roving all over my poor sick body, my body that was still recovering from the last time I'd seen him. I started shaking with fear. He was groping and hurting me again, then he tried to get onto the bed settee with me, and suddenly I could take no more. I started to kick out at him, but he grabbed me even more tightly.

'No, no, please don't,' I cried.

He laughed, and the laugh sounded eerie and menacing. 'Come on,' he urged. 'You know it's good. You know you like me doing it.'

How could he think that? Couldn't he hear me crying out? I hated it passionately. I couldn't *bear* what he did to me.

I struggled with all my might, but he managed to pull my nightie right up and started touching me between my legs, poking his finger inside me and hurting me badly. That horrible whisky smell was on his breath again. I began to sob but my tears didn't seem to make any difference as Uncle Bill continued his onslaught. By this time he was groaning and writhing around on top of me. He grabbed my hand and made me touch him.

'I don't want to,' I cried through my tears. 'I don't want to touch it.'

He wasn't listening; he was past listening. He was pushing my hand up and down on his love toy, his awfulness. Then he took my hand away and I thought it was over – but it wasn't. He fiddled between my legs and then there was that terrible, tearing pain as he pushed himself inside me and began to pound away. He grunted and moaned as he pushed harder and harder, hurting me somewhere deep inside my belly. I sobbed bitterly all the way through, my face turned to the wall, the pain making me want to die. I wanted blackness, nothingness. I wanted not to be able to feel any more.

He was sweating heavily and slobbering all over my face and neck with his fat lips, then with one last grunt he collapsed in a satisfied heap on top of me.

By this time I was numb. I couldn't cry now. It was too bad for tears.

Uncle Bill got up and went into the kitchen. I lay still, unable to move, listening to the sounds of him running the tap to wash his hands, then the cupboard door opening.

When he came back with a glass of juice in his hand, he said, 'I do love you, you know.' That word again: love. This was love? 'You don't know how lucky you are to have me love you as no one else does.' He smiled that awful smile.

'This is our secret and if you ever tell anyone, your punishment will be too frightening to even think about.' He fastened up his shirt and trousers and tucked himself in. 'Anyway, no one would believe you.'

He sounded relaxed and confident and I knew he was right. After all, I had already told and Mum didn't believe me. I wondered what kind of punishment could be worse than what had already happened. Was there anything worse? I couldn't imagine it. If this was lucky, if this was what it was like to be loved, I wished with all of my might that I would become the unluckiest and most unloved child in the world, for the rest of my life.

Uncle Bill grinned and went into the kitchen again. I was completely shattered. I pulled the blankets over my head and tried to shut out the world. Some time later I heard my mother return and I pretended to be asleep. I listened to their muffled whispers in the hall and heard them laughing and joking with each other. I had never felt so alone as I did at that moment. I was utterly isolated, utterly bereft.

When Uncle Bill had gone and everyone else was having tea, I called through and told them I was going to have a bath. The memories of the afternoon's horrors were too much to bear. I couldn't spend the night downstairs in the place where they had happened, so I decided I'd go back to sleep in my own bed afterwards.

In the privacy of the bathroom, my sanctity, I tried desperately to wash away the awful memories of the day. It was sticky between my legs and my private parts were burning really badly, with a pain that seemed worse than last time. My tummy was hurting and felt swollen. My whole body ached where I was bruised from being held down in his firm grip and crushed by his pounding frame. He was a big man, not fat but muscular, much bigger and stronger than my dad.

After the bath I crawled into my own bed, scared, confused and in a great deal of pain. I felt totally alone and broken, like an old discarded toy.

For days after this attack, I refused to leave my room and my dad was very concerned. 'What's up, Cassie?' he asked, sitting on the edge of the bed, stroking the hair back from my forehead. 'You're not yourself at all. Are you really poorly? Tell me how you're feeling. Does it hurt somewhere?'

I nodded my head, tears welling up at his concerned tone. 'Yes, everywhere,' I whispered.

'Why don't you come downstairs and watch some television? Or we could draw.'

I shook my head.

'Is there anything you'd like to eat or drink? Maybe some hot chocolate?'

'I'm OK, thanks.'

I just couldn't tell him anything and it broke my heart that he was being so kind and gentle with me.

'Why are you wasting your time?' Mum snapped at him. 'She's only sulking to get attention.'

She had no idea the trauma I was going through because she didn't care enough to look below the surface. She never once asked me what was wrong and why I was so upset. Maybe I would have been able to tell her if she'd asked the right questions, if she'd encouraged me to open up to her. After all, I'd told her before. But she was happy to let me linger in my bed so long as I kept out of her way and didn't interfere with her precious social life.

Eventually I dragged myself up and back to school again. It was the last term of the year and that was always the best term, with concerts, sports day and the school play. I still didn't feel completely well but I went back so that Uncle Bill couldn't visit any more and try to repeat his horrific attacks.

I tried my hardest not to be in the house when he visited, and for a while I succeeded. I could take the dog out for a long walk, go to Claire's house on Fridays and sometimes on other nights if I argued that we needed to do homework together, or I could disappear off to choir practice. It was inevitable that our paths would cross eventually, but in the meantime Uncle Bill kept demanding of Mum where I was and why he hadn't seen me until she accused me of being rude to him, and ungrateful for all the attention he gave me.

I looked at her and wondered what on earth was going on in her head. I'd told her about the kind of 'attention' Bill gave me and she didn't want to know. Why did she still persist in trying to force us together? I couldn't make head or tail of it.

One evening while I was in my room doing my homework, I heard someone on the stairs and I glanced up nervously. My bedroom door opened and there stood the man I loathed more than any other living being. He grinned. 'Hello, Cassie.'

I sat very still without speaking and hoped I would be safe since the family were all downstairs.

Uncle Bill came over to where I sat writing an essay and placed his hand over my mouth then he bent down to kiss me on the neck.

I jumped up, pushing him away, but he just laughed and stood between me and the door, blocking my escape. My heart was beating hard as all the awful memories came flooding back. I had tried to block them from my mind but they were never far away, making me shudder with revulsion as they came to the surface.

I did tell, I did

He moved forward, pressed his body against mine, then tried to kiss me on the lips. I felt sick and turned my head to the side.

'No one will hear us,' he said. 'They've gone next door to see the new puppy.' Before I had a chance to push past him, he grabbed my hand and thrust it inside his trousers.

I struggled, but he just pushed his body into me, jamming my hand between us.

'Yes, yes,' he slurred, moving himself up and down against me and making the groaning noise I hated so much. I used to hear that noise echoing in my head at night while I lay in bed: in my quiet, dark moments, in my dreams.

As I struggled to get away Bill became more excited. The more I struggled, the more he seemed to like it. I was so petrified that I hadn't uttered a word so far but suddenly he gripped me so tightly that I couldn't help but scream at the top of my voice. He jumped back and I seized my opportunity to run out into the hall. I couldn't decide where to go but, fearful that he was following, I ran into Tom's room and hid down the side of the bed. My heart was pounding as I heard Bill come out onto the landing and hesitate, but then his footsteps trudged slowly down the stairs. He wasn't trying to find me.

Once I was sure the coast was clear, I skipped back into my own room and lay on the bed, feeling shattered by what had happened. My room had always been a refuge before, and now even there wasn't safe. Wherever I was, Bill could always find me and abuse me. There was nowhere he couldn't reach me.

After this last horror, I spent even more time out of the house, walking the dog down to the seafront and staying out for hours on end. I loved the sea. I could just stand and look at the waves and pretend that I was far away from all of this. No one ever asked where I was going or when I would be back. I lived in the same house as them, we sat down to meals together, but otherwise they treated me like an outcast.

I'd restarted violin lessons, and what with them, choir practice and all my household chores, I didn't have much time to reflect, which was fine with me. I didn't want to think about my life. If I didn't think, I could pretend that all was well and things were perfectly fine. I didn't have to think about the uncle who abused me and the mother who hated me so much that she refused to listen to my complaints and protect me from him.

And then a miracle happened. At last God answered my prayers. I heard from Rosie that Mum had fallen out with Uncle Bill's wife Gwen, and as a result Uncle Bill had to promise that he would never come round our house again. I had no idea what the row was about, as Gwen was usually a quiet, mild-mannered lady who I had never heard utter a cross word. Then, when I thought about it some more, I decided it must be because Mum had realised what Bill was doing to me and had belatedly decided to put a stop to it. Surely that must be it?

Mum was sitting on her bed crying as I crept into the room and threw my arms round her neck, overcome with gratitude. Normally I wouldn't have dared to hug her. Whenever I'd tried in the past she'd always pushed me away sharply, but this time I was convinced that she finally believed me about Uncle Bill and that was the reason for her tears. 'Thank you! Thank you for believing me. I knew you would really,' I cried, overjoyed that at last she had taken my word for it and had seen that evil man for what he really was.

Seconds later, I was hurled to the floor and Mum was screaming at me furiously.

'What are you talking about?' She glared at me. 'Of course it had nothing to do with *that*.' She was utterly furious. 'Do you really believe that I cared about what you said? Do you really think that anything you said would have made Bill and me row?' She shook her head in disgust and spat out her words. 'Your feelings and your welfare are the furthest things from my mind right now, you selfish, horrible girl. Get that into your head. I don't care tuppence about you. OK?'

I lay on the floor, stunned.

'Get out of my sight.' She turned her back. 'Don't come near me again.'

I crawled out of the room, completely devastated once more. How could I have been so stupid as to think she had had a change of heart and decided to protect me? She really didn't care. She wasn't anything like all my friends' mothers, who adored them. I was nothing to her. Worse than nothing – she actually hated me.

I heard her sobbing bitterly in her bedroom and wondered what she was so upset about. Maybe she felt bad about the row she'd had with Gwen. I supposed she would miss Uncle Bill, since she seemed to be such great friends with him, but as far as I was concerned it was the best thing that had ever happened in my life. I wasn't safe from my mother's bullying and emotional cruelty but at least I was safe from that monster who had terrified me and hurt me so badly. At least I didn't have to keep looking over my shoulder and wondering if I was safe every time I was left in the house on my own. If I heard a creak on the stairs, it wouldn't be him coming to attack me again.

The relief was so overwhelming that it drowned out any worries about why my mother might be crying in her bedroom and why she hated me. I got down on my knees and thanked God over and over again for rescuing me. I had known all along He would listen and eventually He had. I was safe at last.

Chapter Nine

Although I had lots of other friends, Claire and I were still bestest friends and I still spent every Friday night at hers after the Brigade meetings. We had so much in common that we never ran out of conversation. We chatted about what was happening at school, about other friends there, and about the programmes we watched on television. Claire had a crush on Robert Horton, who played Flint McCullough in the TV series *Wagon Train*. There was a bus driver on her local route who looked just like him so sometimes, after school, we would wait at the top of her road just in case he was driving and she could steal a glimpse of him. My hero was Edd Byrnes, who played Kookie in *77 Sunset Strip*, and I'd style my hair in a ponytail just like the girls in the show. On Saturday mornings, we would go down to Littlewood's department store and try out the pink shiny lipsticks in the cosmetics department or go into the changing rooms to try on new outfits. When I was with her, time flew. I felt like a different person: relaxed, happy, normal. These were the in-between times, the times that kept me sane.

We were similar in lots of ways, but unlike Claire I wasn't good at meeting new people. I tended to distrust all men, except Claire's lovely dad, and I would never stay in a room on my own with a man. If Claire stopped to talk to a family friend in the street, I shrank behind her, anxiously stepping from foot to foot until we moved on. I just didn't feel safe in the company of men. I never knew when I might meet another man like Uncle Bill who might want to do these things to me, and it terrified me.

My relationship with Mum went from bad to worse and I started asking if I could stay at Claire's more and more often. Usually she'd agree because it got me out from under her feet but sometimes she refused, just to spite me, because she didn't want me to enjoy myself. I loved staying there. If I was at Claire's house, I wasn't at mine. Everyone at school knew that Claire's and my friendship was special but no one knew just how much I needed her. Claire was my safety, my soulmate, closer than a real sister could possibly have been.

At the end of our first year together at the secondary modern, disaster struck. Claire's parents announced they were moving home and that the move would take them outside the catchment area for our school. Claire would have to move to a new school and we'd be separated. After they made the announcement I sat in complete shock, unable to speak.

'We've had an idea, though,' Claire's mum said. 'I know your mum has got her hands full with all you kids at home and I wondered if maybe she would let you come and stay with us during the week and you could attend the new school with Claire? Then you could go home at weekends to catch up with your family. It would be like boarding school, except you'd be boarding with us. Would you like that?'

'Oh yes!' I exclaimed immediately, hope springing up in my heart. 'Yes please! I'd love to come and live with you.'

'Maybe Claire could come and stay at your house on Saturday and Sunday and that way the two of you need never be separated. Would you like me to pop round and ask your mum?'

My spirits sank. Reality started to dawn. Mum would never agree. She wouldn't do something that would make me so happy. Besides, who would do all my chores at home? Of course she wouldn't agree.

Still I clung to hope as Claire's mother left the house to go and see my mother. After a while, she returned. She didn't look very happy and I held my breath.

'I asked your mum, Cassie,' she said quietly. 'I explained how close you and Claire are and that I felt this friendship was good for both of you. But I'm afraid she says that she can't spare you at home so the answer is no.'

Claire started to cry and I stood, stock still, flooded with misery. How would I cope without Claire?

'You can still see each other at Brigade on Fridays and maybe your mum will let you stay the weekend,' Claire's mum said hopefully. 'You'll just be at different schools during the week.' She pulled us both over for a hug. 'It won't be so bad. You'll get used to it.'

But it *was* bad. Second year started and I was in mourning. Every break time and every lunchtime I stood at our school gates, crying for my friend. No one could comfort me. No one understood why I needed to see Claire every day. No one understood that life wasn't bearable for me without her around. She was the only person I knew who loved me and made me feel all right about myself. Her constant cheerfulness was the only thing that could break through my depression, and without it I sank deeper and deeper into a hole.

I tried over and over again to get Mum to change her mind but she stuck her heels in and refused. The more I asked her, the more adamant she became.

My teachers became concerned about me because I wasn't eating, wasn't sleeping, wasn't socialising with the other girls, and my grades started to slip. A couple of teachers took me aside and asked if I had any problems, if there was anything they could help with. I told them I just wanted to go and live with Claire and go to her new school with her, but there was nothing they could do. It was my mum's decision where I lived and they couldn't intervene. They thought mine was just the normal reaction of a little girl who'd been separated from her best friend. They didn't know how much I relied on Claire, how unbearable my life was without her.

Eventually, over the months, I got used to being without Claire and I got closer to some other girls. There was Wendy, with whom I'd done confirmation classes, who was a quiet, studious girl, and Maureen, a funny girl who could be naughty at times. But neither of them could make up for the loss of

I did tell, I did

Claire. Our Friday nights just weren't enough to make me feel happy and loved again.

I still had my daydream that the well-dressed man and wife would turn up on our doorstep and claim me as theirs. Occasionally I thought back to the argument in which Mum had told Dad that he had no rights over me. What had she meant by that? Maybe it meant it was true that I was adopted and that my real mother and father were out there somewhere hunting for me. I knew it was only make-believe but I couldn't stop dreaming. It kept me going.

Then, in January of my second year at the secondary modern, came some news that I had been dreading with all my heart and soul. Whatever the row between Mum and Uncle Bill had been about, they had made up.

'Bill's coming round tomorrow,' she said happily over tea one night. 'He's been away on holiday but he's dying to see us so he's coming over as soon as he gets back.'

I froze with fear and my heart started beating hard. What was I going to do? Where would I be safe now? Who would help me? I couldn't understand why God had let this happen. Had he stopped listening to me altogether?

Mum chattered happily throughout the rest of the meal but I couldn't eat, couldn't breathe for terror. I would be at the mercy of evil once again. There was nowhere left I could hide.

Chapter Ten

Mum insisted I had to come straight home from school the next day. There was no way out of it. Uncle Bill was coming for tea and she wanted the whole family at home to greet him.

When the front door was opened and I saw him standing there with his black curly hair, his eyes darting straight over Mum's shoulder to where I stood in the corner, I felt physically sick. I tried to disappear into the wallpaper, to shrink out of sight, but he was coming over, coming my way. I wished I was anywhere but there.

'Hello, Cassie, how are you?' he asked, grinning broadly at me.

My throat closed up so I could barely speak. 'OK,' I mumbled.

'Come and sit down, Bill,' Mum said, gesturing to a chair. 'What can I get you?'

'I've brought presents for everyone,' he said, and it was then I noticed the carrier bags he was holding. 'Who wants theirs first?'

I did tell, I did

'Me!' my sister Anne cried excitedly. He handed her a new skipping rope and a pop-gun that fired a ping-pong ball on a string. Then he walked over to where Tom was sitting and gave him a large coloured ball and a box containing cricket stumps. Tom was thrilled to bits. Then he came towards me. I started shaking. Couldn't they all see how scared I was? I wanted to run from the room before he could reach me, before he got close.

'Here you go, Cassie,' he said. 'This one's for you.' He held out a ribbon for my hair and a little handbag with a brush and comb set inside. 'These will make you even prettier.'

I didn't want his presents, didn't want him to think I was pretty, so I wouldn't take them. I just couldn't. It felt as though he were buying me, paying for the games he made me play. I didn't want to touch anything that he had touched.

'Don't be so rude!' my mother snapped. 'Take those presents straight away. Bill's gone to a lot of trouble to get them for you.'

I stretched out my hand and tried to take them without looking at him, but his thumb brushed my fingers and I flinched. These were the hands that gripped me tightly and held me down, that poked inside my panties, the hands that hurt me.

'Now give him a kiss to say thank you,' Mum ordered. 'Honestly, that girl has no manners whatsoever. Go on!' The last thing I wanted to do was to kiss the man who had hurt me so badly. But she insisted.

I was forced to lean over and brush my lips across Bill's cheek, my whole body shaking with revulsion. There was that familiar whisky smell I hated, the touch of his sweaty skin, the smirk on his face. My stomach turned over.

How could my mother make me kiss him? She *knew* I was terrified of him. I'd told her he touched me between the legs. I'd told her he kissed and hugged me and hurt me. If she didn't want to banish him from our house altogether, why didn't she stop him from seeing me on my own? It's the very least any mother should have done. But she wasn't any mother – she was *my* mother, the woman who for some reason hated me. I was never going to get protection from her.

Bill looked at me. 'I've missed you, Cassie. We'll have to go out together some time soon and catch up.'

I didn't say anything. I couldn't speak. I thought my heart would stop completely if he looked at me one more time. Go out with him? I never wanted to go out with him ever again.

'Cassie, you ungrateful girl. Say thank you very much to Bill for the kind offer.' Still I said nothing, just stared at my feet. My face was burning and I was sure it must be bright scarlet. 'Excuse my rude daughter. She'd love to come out with you, Bill. Just let us know when you want to take her.'

'She's only teasing, aren't you, Cassie?' he chuckled.

Suddenly I couldn't take any more. Mumbling that I had to go to the toilet, I rushed out of the room and ran upstairs. I hurried into the bedroom and shut the door behind me, but I knew I wasn't safe even there. He could come up at any moment. I wasn't safe anywhere any more. I threw myself down on the bed and began to shake convulsively, the memories of all the awful things he had ever done to me and all the pain he had caused me throwing my body into spasms.

He didn't come upstairs that day. I was left to myself, although after he went Mum came up and gave me a huge row for being so rude.

I reverted to my old strategy of trying to avoid being in the house when I knew Bill was coming round. I'd walk the dog for longer and longer stretches of time; I'd stay behind after choir practice; I would even go and help Auntie Mary in her fish and chip shop, peeling potatoes or cleaning the deep-fat fryers – anything that kept me out of the house. But it got harder and harder to predict when he was coming, and Mum tried to arrange his visits so that I'd be there, for some reason. It was as if she was trying to force him upon me.

After he had been back in favour for about a month, he asked if he could take me out for a drive one day. I froze, and my face must have shown the sheer terror I felt, but Mum said, 'That's a good idea. You two go off and have a nice time together.'

I panicked. 'Please, Mum, I've got lots of homework that I have to do by tomorrow. I can't go. Please don't make me.'

'Don't be silly, Cassie. Of course you can take an hour off to spend with your favourite uncle. He's missed you. He's been looking forward to spending time with you.' She gave me a don't-you-argue-with-me look.

'I really can't, Mum. My teacher will be cross. I'll get into trouble at school. Don't make me go.'

'This is ridiculous!' she snapped. 'Poor Bill is standing here offering you a treat and you throw it back in his face. Get out to the car right now. I won't hear another word.'

There was nothing I could do. As we left the house and walked down the path, Uncle Bill took my hand, for all the world as if he were a loving uncle with his favourite niece. He was always telling me I was his favourite: that I was special, that he cared about me, that he loved me. Words, lying words. To me the word 'love' meant something nasty and horrid and evil. The word 'love' was a lie.

Bill led me to the car and helped me into the front seat, his grip vice-like just in case I decided to make a run for it. He wasn't going to let me slip away now. He was going to make sure he had his way.

I didn't know where we were going: didn't know and didn't care. Anywhere was going to be bad. He could have taken me to Heaven on Earth but it would have been Hell for me.

We drove for a long time, much longer than usual. He was talking to me, I think, but I didn't listen and I've got no idea what it was about. There was a rushing sound in my ears and my heart was beating hard. I knew what was about to happen. I knew he was about to hurt me.

Bill was obviously dying to get to our destination because he swore when we came upon a diversion sign in the road. He had no choice but to follow the signs, but shortly after we turned into the new road he pulled up in the middle of nowhere, just by a path that led into a field. What was he doing? What now?

He suddenly lurched towards me and grabbed my leg, pulling it over to his side of the seat, and he began to kiss me roughly, squashing my teeth against my lip. 'Oh, I've missed this. I've missed you,' he slurred, grabbing at my skirt and trying to push his hand inside my panties.

I wanted to cry for him to stop but I couldn't. I was so terrified I couldn't make a sound. I hadn't forgotten the pain of the many times he had abused me before. I prayed that this time he would stop before he hurt me as badly as the other times.

I prayed that God would prevent this happening. After all, I was a good girl. I'd been confirmed now. Why wasn't God listening?

Uncle Bill grabbed my hand and thrust it into his trousers. There were no preliminaries today, no pretence that we were playing a game of 'find the love toy'. He seemed desperate. He was swearing under his breath, and his hands were rough and urgent. He couldn't wait.

Suddenly he pulled my legs apart, yanked my panties to one side, lay on top of me and pushed inside me with a loud grunt. I braced myself for the onslaught of shoving and pushing but this time it was all over in a second and he had collapsed on top of me with a sigh. Was that it? Had God been listening? Was it over already? Could we go home now?

The relief I felt was short-lived. He fastened his trousers again, fumbling with the buttons, then started the car and pulled out onto the road, still driving in the same direction. Why hadn't we turned back towards home? What was going to happen now?

After what seemed like eternity, we drove down a path by a stretch of water, the towpath of a canal or river, although I've got no idea which it was. Then we stopped and he put the car in reverse and drove slowly alongside a boat. A houseboat.

Bill parked carefully and put the brake on, then turned to me with excitement, his face animated. 'We are going to have such fun here,' he grinned. 'There's no one around so we can play games for as long as we want.'

My stomach was knotted so tightly I couldn't move. Bill came round to my side and grabbed my hand to pull me out of the car.

'Don't you want to come and have a look?' he asked, as if I should be excited and eager. Did he really think I enjoyed these games? Did he honestly think they made me happy? Why did he think I cried and screamed and begged him to stop? Was he deaf and blind to my pleas?

'Come on, let's get on board,' he urged.

'I don't like boats,' I said in a small voice, the only one I could manage. I didn't like boats, didn't like his games, didn't like him.

'It'll be all right. I'll look after you,' he told me.

I knew about his kind of looking after and I didn't want it. I wanted to be back at home, in my bedroom, on my own. I looked around, up and down the towpath, but there was no one else in sight. No other boats were moored on that stretch. I was utterly and completely at his mercy. I considered trying to make a run for it, but where would I go? In which direction would I run? Anyway, he was a grown man and would catch me before I got far at all. I was still a skinny little girl and not a fast runner.

The houseboat was brown and a bit grimy. He pushed me up onto the deck then down some wooden steps into a room that had a sort of bed in it. There was nothing else except a bed. I went cold. I suppose I had hoped that there would be very little room in a boat for him to be able to hurt me again, but there was plenty of space in there for him to do whatever he wanted. He sat on the bed and stood me in front of him.

'Take your clothes off,' he ordered, and I began to cry.

I had been trying to teach myself to switch off during his abuse. I don't mean I switched off to what was happening to the extent that I didn't make any memories; that would have been wonderful but I couldn't manage that. Instead I taught myself to concentrate on something else, such as the sea. I would think about waves washing up on the seashore, the shushing sound as they pulled back along the sand, and their rhythmic, time-less movement. It didn't stop the fear, but it made it bearable. I tried to shut myself off in my head, to put all the horrid nasti-ness into a box and keep it there with the lid firmly on. If I could learn to do it really well, I hoped I'd be able to cut off from what was happening to me. But when he made me take my clothes off, I felt so exposed that I couldn't switch off, couldn't pretend I was anywhere else but there. Present. In that moment. I was a small, helpless child.

'Get them off!' he ordered again, and I obeyed because there was nothing else I could do. Slowly I unbuttoned my school cardigan and shirt, pulled my vest over my head, then sat down on the edge of the bed to remove my socks and shoes. All the time Bill was staring at me, touching himself and making groaning noises in his throat.

'Lovely,' he leered. 'You're lovely and you're all mine.'

I couldn't bring myself to remove my panties, but Bill came over and ripped them off then pushed me back on the bed, forcing my legs apart.

'Oh. I love you. You know that, don't you? I've missed you and missed our games. I know you must have missed this too, haven't you?'

Before I could answer, there was the sudden horrendous pain again. Pain like I had never felt before in my young life. He kept pushing and pushing himself inside me and I was trying to scream that it hurt but no sound came out of my mouth. The love toy had become an evil monster controlled by him, my godfather, the man they called Uncle Bill. How could he do this to me? Why? What had I done to deserve this?

I had stopped crying. I kept my eyes closed and tried to stop breathing altogether. I stopped being, stopped living. I was a thing, an object, not a person. On and on it went without respite, for longer than it ever had before.

When it was over, the man who professed to love me pushed me away so hard that I fell onto the floor. He was swearing and trying to get his trousers back on and he couldn't do the buttons up for some reason.

'Get up, get over here and button these up!' he shouted.

I shook my head. I couldn't touch his sweaty, smelly trousers. I couldn't move. I was hurting and scared. Why should I do anything to help him when all he ever did was hurt me?

But when he ordered me again, my courage failed and I got up and did his bidding with shaking fingers. My whole body shook after our 'games'. It was as if my muscles went into a spasm of revulsion. My teeth were chattering, my legs felt like jelly and there were palpitations in my chest. Every part of my body was protesting at the way it had been treated.

In the car on the way home, I sat mute, huddled, with my arms round myself. Bill looked over and grinned. 'We'll have to go to the boat again really soon, Cassie. But remember this is our secret. You can't tell anyone. You know what will happen if you do.' He left the threat hanging in the air. 'Besides, no one will believe you anyway.'

He didn't have to remind me of that. I knew that already. I had told Mum and I hadn't been believed.

Uncle Bill dropped me off outside our front door, patting my knee and smiling as though we'd just been out for a treat together, like the zoo or a funfair. 'See you again soon, Cassie,' he said. 'Tell your mum I had to dash but that I'll see her next time.'

I went into the house and straight up to the bathroom, where I locked the door behind me. No one shouted up to ask if I was OK or if I'd had a good time. I ran some water in the bath, took my clothes off then I climbed into the water and scrubbed and scrubbed myself until I bled. I wanted to erase any last trace of Bill's smell from my skin, get rid of any lingering stickiness from the yucky stuff he left inside me.

I didn't go downstairs for tea and no one came up to ask why not. I just dried myself and went straight to bed. I prayed to God yet again to rescue me from my uncle and then I cried myself to sleep, muffling the sound of my sobs in the pillow. I must have been the loneliest girl in the world at that point. No one was listening. No one cared.

After the first visit to the houseboat, things settled into a routine. Bill arranged with my mum that he would pick me up after school three nights a week, when I didn't have choir practice or Girls' Brigade. I was safe on Tuesdays and Fridays but not the rest of the week.

'She needs a hand with all those books to carry,' he said. 'And I've got the car so I'm happy to do it.'

On the way home, he would pull off the road into the bluebell wood, telling me we had to play our secret game. This might be pushing his love toy inside me, or making me lick it or forcing my hands round it until the white stuff squirted out. We'd be late home, but Bill would always have some explanation for Mum – an errand he had to do, something he needed to pick up, or the car needing petrol. Not that she ever asked where we had been. It didn't matter to her. She wouldn't have noticed.

We went to the houseboat most weekends, and then there was more time for his sick games. He would tell me that the love toy became very angry if it wasn't treated well. Treating it well, I had learned, meant touching and stroking it until it became hard then, the worst part of all, licking it until he said it was clean.

I never looked at it. Never looked at him. I did my best to find a safe place in my head where I could forget about the ugly purple piece of flesh in my hands or in my mouth or between my legs. I tried to forget about the grimacing, sweating face looming over me and the fat lips covering my face and neck with their slobber.

After we began to go to the houseboat on Saturdays, Bill made Mum tell Claire's mum that I couldn't stay over on Friday nights any more because he wanted me up bright and early, ready for him to pick me up for a full day of abuse. I took this new blow without complaint. I had no power to affect anything about my life any more. I was utterly powerless. Some Saturdays he would bring a picnic with him, or he would stop and get some fish and chips at a nearby shop, but I could never eat. I was too scared and tense to eat, too sickened by what he did to me. We never stayed overnight but we could be there all day. Long horrible days that left me in a lot of pain.

Life was utterly unbearable. The in-between bits were very rare now. I was sleepwalking from one assault to the next. I hardly ever saw Claire, except at the Girls' Life Brigade meeting when we were busy and didn't have time to talk, then I would have to say goodbye to her at the bus stop and go straight home afterwards. At the age of thirteen she left the Brigade when schoolwork got too demanding, and I did the same. The hope seemed to have disappeared from my life altogether and I thought God had gone with it. My life was a sham. A painful, scary sham.

It was as though everything I'd ever had had been stolen from me. I was living a lie, pretending to everyone around me, lying about where I'd been because the truth was just too awful. I never cried any more. I just went through the motions of going to school, doing my work, then walking out the school gates to where Uncle Bill's black Austin was parked. It never occurred to me to make an excuse and say that I had to stay behind late or something. The caretaker locked the gates at 4.30 anyway, so it wouldn't have worked.

If it was raining, my friends would say, 'Aren't you lucky having someone to give you a lift home?' Not many of their parents had cars in those days. I'd just look at them and think how little they knew me. Bill would never get out of the car to greet me. He'd just wait till I got in, then he'd start the car and drive off to the woods.

When I look back, I don't know how I survived. But I was just surviving, not living. I couldn't share what was happening to me. I was twelve years old and I felt like the walking dead.

I became more and more introspective. While my friends liked Elvis Presley, I preferred sad ballads like Patsy Cline's 'Walkin' After Midnight' and Carl Smith's 'Why? Why?' I started reading romantic novels and poetry because they took me outside my own head to a make-believe place far away. Friends invited me to parties but I always refused, embarrassed because I didn't have anything to wear, and didn't know how to be around boys. What would I say to them? What would they expect of me?

Ellen and Rosie were working in the local hospital and both had boyfriends, so I watched them dressing up in the big full skirts of the period, giggling as they checked their makeup and pulled on stilettos. Tom left school at fifteen and joined the Marine cadets and I liked to help him clean the brass buttons and white belts of his uniform. He was the only one I felt remotely close to. I loved him and I think he cared about me as well, but we never had a conversation about what was really going on in the house and I couldn't ever have told him about my misery. Anne was still the baby of the family, but I began to worry that Uncle Bill might turn his attentions to her one day. I thought about warning someone, telling them to keep an eye on him – but how could I, without telling what he was doing to me? So I said nothing.

I hadn't had any sex education at school but I knew what Bill was doing was wrong. My friends had talked about kissing boys and 'playing around' but I didn't know what 'playing around' meant. I thought it must be fun and what was happening to me was anything but fun. One day Wendy told us that her mum and dad were having a baby and she exclaimed that she hadn't realised they had sex. Maureen laughed and began to describe graphically what happens when a baby is created. It was only then I realised that what Uncle Bill was doing to me was grown-up sex, the kind that makes babies. Up till then I'd been unsure and confused.

One day we were lying on the bed in the houseboat after he had raped me, when he said something that shattered me: 'If you told anyone about us now, they'd think you must have been enjoying it all this time. They'd think you agreed, that you wanted to be my girlfriend. Have you ever thought about that?'

The thought that anyone could believe I enjoyed his attentions had never occurred to me. Of course it hadn't.

'They'll think you must have loved it. That you made advances to me and flirted with me. You're the guilty one and

I'm innocent. They'd probably send you away to a home, a place where you could play these games all the time.'

I thought about what he said and decided it was probably true. I'd been playing games with Bill since the age of seven and I was now a teenager. He first forced himself inside me when I was eleven. If I hadn't wanted to do it, everyone would assume I'd just have stopped. They wouldn't understand how he drained the will to resist from me, drained the will to live. He persuaded me that everyone would believe I'd been in love with him and it was all my own fault. *Was* it my own fault?

Now I felt guilty as well as dirty. That is, when I felt anything at all.

Chapter Eleven

When I was about fourteen, my Nana C, Mum's mum, came to stay with us. She had been very poorly and Mum was the only family she had so, reluctantly, Mum agreed she could move in. We didn't have a spare bedroom upstairs but a bed was put into the back room of the ground floor of the house and she was installed in there with all her bits and pieces.

I was pleased when she came as I was very fond of her and she was kind to me whenever Mum wasn't around. Mum told me that it was my responsibility to look after Nana. This gave her an excuse to exclude me from family outings to the fair or to the beach, but I didn't mind because I was much happier staying at home with Nana.

We had secrets between us, secrets that I was happy to keep. Good secrets. For example, my mother thought Nana was bedridden. In order to be allowed to move in, she'd had to pretend she couldn't walk and I was the only one who was in on the secret that she actually could, albeit slowly. When the family went out for the day, I'd watch out of the window as they drove out of sight over the bridge at the end of our road, then I'd give Nana the all clear.

'Have they gone yet?' she would ask. 'Have they gone over the bridge?'

When she was sure they were out of the way, she would get out of bed and hobble through to join me in the kitchen. On these occasions we would sit together and she would tell me stories about the war. Not scary stories, but nice ones about the sing-songs she and her neighbours had in the air-raid shelters. She told me about her husband, my Mum's dad, who went missing during the First World War and how much in love they had been. And she made me laugh with tales of her escapades when she was young. Once when she was helping at the local hospital, Queen Elizabeth the Queen Mother was visiting. Nana was running late and was still on her hands and knees drying the floor as the royal visitors approached. Not wanting to get caught, she crawled under a table and had to stay there until they had gone. She fell about laughing as she described peering out at their shoes as they chatted away unawares.

When we were alone together we would make jam tarts and eat them all before anyone returned, so as not to give the game away. We would sit out in the garden and play with my dog. Sometimes we would just sit together and say nothing. But we were always sure to get Nana back in bed before anyone returned, and they never guessed our secret.

These were good times, in-between times that helped me to get through all the rest. It never occurred to me to tell Nana about Uncle Bill, though. What if he was right and she thought it was all my own fault? I couldn't bear her to think badly of me. It was too awful to contemplate.

I lived inside my own protective bubble and I wouldn't let anyone else in because I didn't want them to see the real me. I thought there was something wrong with me and I felt ashamed. I was growing up with no help or comfort from Mum, the person who should have been guiding me, and I felt mentally and emotionally let down by her. The scars from the sexual abuse were getting deeper and deeper. I became more practised at putting the bad things away in a box and trying not to look at them, but the more I hid them from the light, the more I came to feel that I couldn't let anyone else close in case they saw what I was really like and despised me for it.

After about six months Nana moved out of our place and went to live with a friend of hers, and I missed her badly. It had been lovely having a secret ally in the house.

At school my friends starting talking about what they wanted to do for a career. I thought I might like to be a journalist, going all over the world and reporting from trouble spots, or maybe a teacher, because all the teachers I had known had been kind, caring people who had shown concern for me. I would pretend in quiet moments that I was already a grown-up person with a career, off interviewing famous people or teaching my class, and then I could feel nice, like a good person.

The rest of the time I felt not nice, dirty, ashamed of how my life was, both at home with Mum and when I was out with Uncle Bill. I didn't feel I could possibly be a 'nice' person then.

I would try hard not to be conspicuous, try to fade into the background. When people looked at me, could they see the truth? The dirty, nasty reality?

When I was fifteen, my periods started and I was so naïve that I had no idea what they were. No one had ever thought to tell me, so when I rushed up to the bathroom with pains in my tummy and found that I was bleeding, bleeding a lot, I panicked. Was I dying? Had something happened to me because of what Uncle Bill did? I was terrified. The pain was one thing; I often had cramping pains in my belly after the abuse. And I had bled the first time I was with Bill, but I knew this was different. This bleeding was heavy and I was scared. But who could I talk to?

The only person I could ask was my brother Tom. I knew he would help; he would know what to do. Thank God he was in the house that day. I called him and he came to the bathroom door.

'Tom, I don't know what to do. I'm bleeding. From my private parts.' I thought maybe he would call an ambulance for me. 'Am I dying? Or do you think I am having a baby? I've read that you bleed when you have a baby.'

I wrapped a towel round myself and let him into the room. He smiled and gave me a hug. 'It's OK. This happens when a girl grows up. It's the start of you being a woman.' He stroked my back, comforting me. 'Of course you're not having a baby. You have to have sex to become pregnant.'

Now I was really scared. He thought he was reassuring me, a naïve child, but I wasn't reassured at all. I had had sex, hadn't

I did tell, I did

I? Awful, horrific sex. He had no idea the terrors I had endured. Maybe they had made me pregnant?

Tom went downstairs to tell Mum what had happened to me and came back up again soon after with a bandage and a huge pad-like sanitary towel. There were no tampons in those days. During our periods, we walked around as if we had bricks between our legs.

'Did you tell Mum?' I asked him.

'Yeah, that's why she gave me these things.' He handed them over.

Mum left it to my teenage brother to explain to me that periods were something that happened monthly, and to give advice on how to deal with them. Surely any other mother would have at least come upstairs to offer comfort instead of leaving it to her teenage son – but mine was far from being a natural mother.

I washed myself, worked out how to assemble the sanitary garment and went back into my bedroom to study. I was still scared that I might be pregnant, but as the days went by and a baby didn't come out I began to believe Tom, that it was just a part of growing up.

The next time I went out with Uncle Bill, I was still bleeding. I told him that I had started my periods. Surely he couldn't abuse me then? He'd have to leave me alone, wouldn't he? Otherwise, he'd get blood all over him.

'Well, we'll just have to be happy playing other games,' he said, sounding disappointed.

Happy? I thought, aghast. Who on earth was happy?

'We can find other ways to make up for the grown-up sex. We can't have that any more,' Bill continued.

The games were different that day, more hurried, as though he was annoyed with me. But that was fine by me, because it was over more quickly. After he had satisfied himself, he looked deep in thought.

'We'll have to be inventive. We can still have lots of fun and find other ways to enjoy the games,' he said. 'But we can't risk you getting pregnant. Can't have that.' I had really thought that he would stop making me do these things, now that my periods had started. But it seems he had other plans.

Lots of women complain about their periods but they were a good thing for me. I only wish they had started a few years earlier and they could have spared me a lot of misery. But at fifteen, at last I had a reprieve of sorts. Bill would continue to abuse me in every other way he could think of, but we didn't have 'grown-up sex' any more. I hated the other things he made me do too, but nothing was quite as bad as the pain of feeling him pounding away inside me, raping me, invading me.

Chapter Twelve

There was a new sound in our house when I was fifteen: the sound of babies crying. Mum had applied to be a foster mother and we had a string of young babies through the door who needed to be looked after for a few weeks as they awaited a decision about where their permanent home was to be. Some of them were on their way to adoptive parents, while others had been removed from their families and placed in council care because they were felt to be unsafe at home. The irony of this did not escape me. Somehow Mum had passed all the council tests and proved herself a caring, fit mother of young children. If only they knew what sort of mother she had been to me!

As with Bobby, my little dog, a lot of the unpleasant chores fell to me. Rinsing out soiled nappies then running them through the mangle was added to the list of my other responsibilities around the house, along with meal preparation, changing the beds, scrubbing and polishing. Mum would sit with a clean, gurgling baby on her lap whenever a health visitor came round and then as soon as the door was shut and a nappy needed to be changed she would hand the child over to me. I wasn't sure why she took these babies in until I realised that she was paid. She didn't care about these babies at all; she was only doing it for the money.

I still sang in the choir, and still saw Uncle Bill about four times a week. During the in-between times, which were very few. I worked hard at developing my world of make-believe, in which I could pretend he had never touched me and I had never felt those awful ashamed feelings. I was trying to be a normal, busy teenager, just like all my friends … only they didn't have a big dark secret locked in a box inside their head.

At the age of fifteen I was selected, along with five other girls in my school, to be the first pupils at a secondary modern to take O levels. It was a great honour, although as was to be expected Mum didn't recognise it as such. I wanted to do well but, what with the treatment I received at home and the sexual abuse I was enduring on a regular basis, I didn't have time for any extra studying and couldn't keep up with the work. I began to suffer from severe headaches and one of my teachers suggested that I should go to my doctor.

I went to the surgery and broke down in tears when the doctor asked me what was wrong. What could I say? I told him about the pressure I was under to do well in my exams, and how miserable I felt in general – but I didn't tell him the real reasons why. He was concerned and caring, but didn't push the issue, and I left the surgery with a prescription for benzodiazepines, which I thought were headache pills. I'd never even heard of tranquillisers at that age. I trusted my doctor so I started taking the pills and, sure enough, the headaches became less intense and less frequent. Life was slightly easier and I felt that I just might be able to cope after all, although my head felt a bit fuzzy and my thinking was clouded. When the exams came around, though, I found myself staring miserably at the papers. The upshot was that I failed all five of them.

I was devastated because in the back of my mind I still had the idea that I wanted to be a journalist, and I knew I needed good exam results for this. There was no question of a re-sit, though. My life wasn't my own. I may have been allowed to make decisions for myself once, when I chose not to take the Eleven Plus re-sit, but the choice of my career was apparently Mum's, and she had decided that I should train to be a nurse. She enrolled me on a pre-nursing course at a college a train ride away, to start in the autumn of 1961.

I was sad to leave school at the end of the summer term but my friends all promised to stay in touch. Mum arranged a summer job for me in an electronics factory so that I could earn my keep during the holidays. I was to work on the shop floor, putting components together for the defence industry. Mum and I were sitting in the kitchen one day working out how much of my wages I needed to keep for bus tickets and expenses and how much I should hand over to her, when Uncle Bill arrived.

I tried to leave the room, making the excuse that I had to take the dog for a walk, but Mum wouldn't let me.

'Don't be so rude. We've got a guest. Stay and talk to him,' she ordered.

Some guest! I thought guests were supposed to be people we liked, instead of the reason for everything that was nasty, horrible, scary and painful in my life. But I couldn't say any of this, of course, and he knew I wouldn't. I was too scared to tell.

Mum explained to Bill what we had been talking about, and he came up with an offer that chilled my blood.

'I'll take her to the factory,' he said, looking at me. 'I could collect her as well. I've got nothing else on at the moment.'

'Oh, that will be good, won't it?' Mum said, delighted that a solution had been found that would save her money. 'Isn't that kind of Bill? Say thank you to your uncle.'

Why would I say thank you? He was only giving himself more opportunity to hurt and abuse me. Why would I thank him for that?

It was all decided. He would collect me in the mornings and take me to work and then, just to make my day even less bearable, he would pick me up and bring me home at the end of the day.

'No problem,' he continued, obviously very pleased with himself. 'I might have to make a short detour on the way home sometimes if I have to run errand or two.' He tried to catch my eye but I wouldn't look at him. All I could do was sit there miserably as he and Mum collaborated to arrange my summer of abuse.

My days at the factory job were made bearable by a girl I met called Katie, who was going to be starting the same pre-nursing course as me in September. I'd been apprehensive about starting somewhere new because of my natural shyness, and because of the secret I carried round with me, but her friendship made it all much more bearable.

But then there were the long hours of abuse I had to put up with on the way home from the factory – either in the car, in a field or on the houseboat. I didn't struggle now. I just switched off my thoughts and did whatever he wanted, trying not to feel, not to be present. I didn't get raped because he was worried I would get pregnant – that was one thing – but he still hurt, disgusted and humiliated me in all sorts of nasty, despicable ways.

September came and as soon as I started at the college I met a lovely crowd of girls and new friendships came effortlessly. I soon became very close to Katie. We shared the same sense of humour, teasing each other about boys and comparing notes about our tutors and course work. We got close on a deeper level as well. She told me all about her home life with her father, who was a dentist, her mum, who sounded really nice, and one sister. One day, in the midst of a heart to heart, I found myself on the verge of telling her about Uncle Bill. My life was so busy since starting the pre-nursing course that I only saw him at weekends, but I still had to go with him to the houseboat and put up with whatever disgusting things he wanted to do to me that day.

I looked into Katie's warm, compassionate face and considered the words I would use. By now I knew that what he did to me was rape and sexual abuse. I knew it was wrong and criminal. But I still feared that people would consider me an accomplice. Surely, they would think, I must have wanted it to happen, encouraged it even? Otherwise, why had I put up with it for the last nine years, since the age of seven? Bill kept reminding me that everyone would think I had instigated it. 'What do you think people would think of you?' he would say. I believed him, that they would be suspicious about why I hadn't told anyone during this time.

Of course, I *had* told – but I'd told the wrong person. My mother.

There was nothing I could do except keep myself as busy as possible so that I had no time to see Bill, no time to think. I volunteered to be on the entertainment committee at college and was soon organising dances, day trips, rag days and all kinds of fun events. On Friday nights I sang with a local group that toured the youth clubs in our area, then Katie and I usually met each other on Sundays after I had been to church, or whenever I wasn't at the dreaded houseboat. I felt I was deceiving her somehow when we chatted about boys we were attracted to and plotted how to bump into them accidentally on purpose or make sure they attended a dance we were planning to be at. How could I consider going out with a boyfriend? How could I think of getting married?

But when I fell in love, I realised it's not something you can stop if you try. It just happens and you are powerless against it. The strange thing for me was that the boy I fell in love with was someone I had known when we were much younger, someone the same age as my brother Tom. He was Uncle Bill's son

Steve. We had played together as children. He used to come to the motorbike rallies, where he chatted to Tom and the two of them would gang up to tease me. We lost touch for a few years after Gwen and my mother fell out but met up again at a family party when I was sixteen. I felt shy with him at first because he was very good-looking and I was immediately attracted to him. We sat and talked in a corner of the hall and I realised he was a really nice person as well. When he asked if I would like to see him again, I couldn't believe he was interested in me in a boyfriend-girlfriend sort of way. He wanted to go out with me! I said yes straight away, unable to believe my luck.

On our first date we walked to a favourite spot of his, a castle that was down the hill from where he lived. As we walked, Steve reached for my hand and I was filled up with happiness. Our times together were either at the castle or sometimes he would come to the house, and my mother seemed OK about this. We would sit cuddled up together and play records on my Dansette record player. One day, when he hadn't been able to come over, I realised how much I missed him and it dawned on me that I had fallen in love with him. It was different from anything I had ever felt before. It was good, clean and gentle. We kissed but nothing more, and that was just fine with me.

The next time we met he told me how much he had missed me. 'I want us to be together for ever, Cassie,' he said. 'I love you and want to be with you always.'

I was in heaven! He wanted me. He wanted to be with me just because he loved me. I was the happiest girl alive.

It was unthinkable that I would see Uncle Bill while dating his son so I went out of my way to avoid him. I was at college every day and I shut myself in my bedroom every night to study; on Fridays I sang with the band and then at weekends I went out with Steve. I tried my hardest not to think about Bill and all the evil things he had done to me. I didn't want those memories to taint the happiness I was feeling, but it was difficult. I did wonder what would happen if Steve and I got married. Would Bill have to come to the wedding? I also worried that he might tell Steve about our 'relationship', make him believe that it was all my fault. But then I convinced myself that Steve knew me, the real me, so he would know it wasn't true. He was a kind, loving boy and we seemed to understand each other. I knew he'd had an unhappy home life as well, and although neither of us went into detail about our childhoods we shared enough to feel a strong bond.

And so, we fell in love. Young love, the first love of my entire life. We planned ahead, life was wonderful and I thought we would stay together forever. These were the happiest months of my life. Nothing and nobody could spoil them.

At the end of the first year of college, all of us nursing students were posted to a city hospital for the summer to do some practical work. We would have to board in the hospital concerned and I was dreading it, first and foremost because it would make it impossible to see Steve, but also because my bedroom at home was my sanctuary, the only place where I felt relatively safe. Bill had only tried to abuse me there once and it hadn't worked because I screamed, so he never tried it again.

I did tell, I did

Katie was posted to the same hospital as me, which was a relief, and at least part of the time we were there was fun. We went to barbecues with some police cadets we'd met; we had coffee in a real coffee-house and mixed with proper nurses; and I met some wonderful people, both patients and staff. But the work in the wards was hard. This was the era of matrons, when the wards were ruled with rods of iron. No one spoke unless spoken to, we weren't allowed to wear makeup and we had the most awful, unflattering nursing uniforms that had ever been seen.

My first placement was a male orthopaedic ward. Here I was subjected to what the male patients saw as a bit of harmless fun when, one by one, they asked me to hold their private parts while they used the urine bottle or to pat them dry after a blanket bath, despite the fact that they were perfectly capable of doing so themselves. This brought memories of Uncle Bill's games flooding into my head and I found it utterly unbearable. I told the matron I couldn't cope and she didn't ask me why; I think she assumed that I was a little immature and perhaps something less 'hands on' might be better to begin with. I was moved to the physiotherapy department until they could find another ward placement for me.

There was an amazing physiotherapist working there who was totally blind. Everyone loved him because he was funny, clever and excellent at his job, so I enjoyed being in that department, but it was only a short time before I was moved again, this time to a children's ward. Shortly after I arrived there, a twelve-year-old boy died and I sobbed my heart out.

I couldn't cope at all, and the ward sister threw me off the ward.

The following day I was summoned to the matron's office. She was very kind but said she felt I was not cut out for nursing and asked if I had thought of another career. I tried to explain to her, between sobs, that nursing was my mother's choice, and that I was afraid of letting her down. I couldn't go home early, having failed again. What would she say? What would she do?

The matron said that I might make a good nurse one day, but not yet. She felt I was too immature to handle the pressures at that time, and she suggested that I ring my mother and explain. With a heavy heart I rang home. At first there was silence as I relayed the news, then the storm broke.

'Who do you think you are, making a decision to come home? Who gives you the right to make that decision?' Mum was angrier than I had heard her for a long time. 'Do you enjoy hurting me? Yes, you do. You enjoy letting me down. You must, as that's all you ever do!'

Before I had a chance to defend myself, she continued: 'How much more of a failure are you going to be?'

I didn't reply. What could I say?

'If you come home early, I'll have nothing to do with you, ever again,' she growled down the phone. And then she hung up on me.

I was on my own, miles from home, distressed that I had failed in my course, and feeling as though I was destined always to be a failure. She didn't have to rub it in because I was thinking all the same things myself. A normal mother might have offered comfort, might have said, 'Don't worry, darling. We'll think of a solution to this problem. Just come home and we'll sort it out.' But the mother I had would never say anything like that. She didn't care if I was upset, and wouldn't dream of offering comfort.

I would have loved to phone Steve, but in those days his family didn't have a telephone in their home. It was the thought of seeing him that helped me to get through that day, though. The only positive thing about having to leave the course was that I would be able to see him soon.

The next day I caught a train home. Mum was sitting outside in the garden and I decided to go out and see her straight away, in the vain hope that her anger would have diminished overnight.

'Hello, I'm home!' I called, bracing myself for a stream of invective about how selfish I was and how I had ruined her life. But no, it was to be the silent treatment. She didn't speak to me. No one spoke to me. Ellen was just heading off to work, while Rosie and Tom were out. Anne looked up at me and mouthed 'You're in trouble' then looked away.

I went up to my room and unpacked, then I decided to go and see Steve. I couldn't wait to see him. He would understand. He would sympathise. He would look after me and tell me he loved me and that he was glad I was back home again.

I caught the bus to his house and knocked on the door. Gwen, his mother, answered.

'Is Steve here?' I asked, smiling brightly.

She gave me a strange look. 'You can't see him,' she told me.

I hesitated for a moment, confused. What did she mean? 'I've just got back from my nursing course and wanted to say hello. Is he in?'

'I'm afraid you can't see him any more,' Gwen told me firmly. 'Whatever you had between you, it's over. You mustn't come round here any more.'

I didn't understand. I knew he was at home because his bike was in the front garden, so I shouted out, 'Steve? It's me, Cassie. What's going on?'

There was a pause then I heard him call out: 'Mum, let her come through.'

What happened next broke my heart. I ran to him, expecting that he would open his arms and give me a hug, but he didn't move. I looked at his face and could see he had been crying. Whatever was wrong? Why was this kind, wonderful boy crying? Who had hurt him?

I threw my arms around his neck but he reached up and pulled my hands away.

'I can't see you any more,' he said in a soft voice. 'I have to break up with you. I do love you but I have to end it. I'm so sorry.'

He began sobbing and I started crying as well. I just couldn't understand why he was saying this and I needed to know.

'What's wrong, Steve? I love you and you say you love me.' I could hardly speak through my tears. 'Please tell me what's wrong. If you love me, why are you finishing with me?'

'I can't tell you. I *won't* tell you,' he said, then he pushed me away and ran from the room in tears. I tried to follow but Gwen

I did tell, I did

stepped in the way and asked me to leave. It was then I noticed that she was crying as well.

I had no choice. The door was opened for me, so I stepped out and walked down the path. My world had collapsed around me and I didn't know why. All I knew was that the best thing in my life was over.

I sat down on the pavement outside his house. I must have sat there for hours, hoping that he would come out and talk to me, that everything would be all right again. But he didn't. Eventually, as it got dark, I realised there was no use in waiting any longer and I went home to the house where no one was speaking to me. I had nowhere else to go.

My mind was in turmoil. Nothing made sense. If he loved me, why had he finished with me? And if he wanted to finish with me, why had he seemed so upset about it?

The next few days were empty and overwhelmingly sad. I was desperate to go back to Steve's house again to try and make him talk to me and explain what was going on, but I had no money for the bus fare. I considered walking but it was a long way and he might not have agreed to see me. Anyway, I got a sense that it would be futile. His decision, for whatever reason, was final. He was too nice a person to mess me around. It was definitely the end.

The pain I felt was physical, a harsh pain in the pit of my stomach. I curled up on my bed, hurting too much to move. There was nothing I could do. Once again I was powerless. Once again I was the loneliest person in the world.

Chapter Thirteen

Just before the end of the summer holidays, a few weeks after Steve had finished with me, the matron of the training hospital phoned to say that my written exam results had come in and that I had done well. She suggested that I should continue my nursing course but just delay the practical side that I had found so difficult to cope with. She didn't want me to give up entirely, she said.

I didn't want to go back to nursing but I knew Mum would try to force me to. I felt so devastated about breaking up with Steve that I was almost beyond caring about my future, but the one thing I knew was that I couldn't face going back to working on hospital wards again. I decided to try and have a chat with Dad about my future.

What I would really have liked to do would be to change to a journalism course at the same college. Lots of students changed direction after the first year. In fact, I had heard of one student who was allowed to change course without taking entrance exams because she had done so well in her end-of-year exams. So I thought that, as my exam results had been good, they might accept me. I mentioned this to Dad and he agreed that it sounded like a good idea, but at that point Mum came into the room.

I told her what I had decided. I told her that I didn't think I would ever be ready to study nursing and that I was keen to study journalism. I told her that Dad agreed it was a good idea.

Mum raised herself up to her full height and screamed at me. 'What right do you think he has to agree with you?' She was looking at Dad with an expression that I couldn't interpret. 'He has no rights over you. Only I have!'

I frowned. There was that strange jibe that she had used before over the grammar school decision. 'What do you mean, Dad has no rights? I don't understand. Of course he has rights.'

She was seething with rage. 'How dare you question me!' I'd come home from my nursing course a failure and now I was trying to defy her. I don't think she had ever been angrier with me than she was at that point. 'Ask him!' she screamed at me, pointing to my dad. 'Ask him what I mean.'

I was confused. I looked at my beloved dad, and I'll never forget the pain I saw in his eyes. He was in pieces. He looked totally distraught.

'What does she mean, Dad?' I asked. 'Why is she saying such awful things? I don't understand.'

He looked as if he was trying to hold back tears, which scared and confused me even more.

'You have every right to help me. You're my dad!' I insisted.

Then came the bombshell. He spoke very quietly, as if he didn't want me to hear the words. 'That's just it, love – she's right.' He was looking at Mum with a curious expression I'd never seen before. 'I have no rights over you because I'm not your dad, I'm not your real father.'

I stood still, the words echoing in my ears. What did they mean? Why would he say that? If he wasn't my dad, who was? I think I asked that, in a very small voice.

'Bill,' Mum screamed at me. 'Bill is your dad!'

Uncle Bill, my godfather, the man who abused me? Could he really be my father? I felt sick and began to shake. The evil monster who raped me over and over again was my dad? But I'd told her about what he did to me and she did nothing to stop it. I refused to believe he could be my father. I wouldn't believe it. It was bad enough that *anyone* could subject me to the evil that he subjected me to. But he was responsible for me being born? He was my biological father? This made his actions thousands of times worse. A father, a natural father, would never hurt me. A natural father would have protected me and kept me safe. But a natural father Bill was not.

I felt ill, and my head was hurting with a pain that scared me. How many more shocks could I take? I was still reeling from Steve breaking off our relationship. And then, yet another realisation hit me like a ton weight. The most shattering realisation of all. If it was true that Bill was my father, then the boy I had fallen in love with, who had broken my heart, was my brother.

I ran out of the room and up to the bathroom, where I was violently sick.

Things were beginning to make sense now. They had obviously decided to tell Steve the truth and then leave him to tell me. But he couldn't, he was hurting too much. He *had* to break up with me. It *had* to end. I could see that now.

The only good thing out of all of this, something I was so relieved about later, was that we had never been lovers. Our love was so special, he asked nothing physical of me. Our love was pure. Our love was wonderful. But our love was wrong. And now it was over.

Lots of other things began to make sense now – if sense is the right word. Uncle Bill had often said while he was raping or abusing me that he had the right to do it, and I never knew what he meant at the time. Of course he didn't have the right – no one has that right – but I could see now why he had said it. The jibes that I had listened to for years, in which Mum said that Dad had no rights over me, again made sense now.

To my mind, my real 'father' would always be the man who had brought me up and looked after me through my childhood, the man who made me a pink doll's cot out of tomato boxes. He wasn't the man who abused, destroyed and terrified me, leaving me feeling dirty and ashamed. A man who steals your childhood is not a father. He is evil.

I didn't know the word 'incest' at the age of seventeen. I'm glad I didn't. I was suffering enough and didn't need another thing to feel dirty and ashamed about. But incest it was. Why on earth hadn't Mum tried to stop me going out with Steve? I didn't dare ask her, but all I can assume is that she wanted to cause me pain. She knew the truth would come out eventually, and she wanted me to be unhappy.

For the rest of the summer I was lost in my own heartache. It wasn't just this revelation about my birth, but also the pain of loss, loss of the love I had had. I couldn't get my head around what had happened. For some reason I felt ashamed of how I had hurt my half-brother. Ashamed that I had been treated so badly by Uncle Bill, the man who it now seemed was my father. What an awful person I must be to have been treated this way. It must all be my fault.

Mum had always told me that I was to blame for all the pain she and our family were suffering. This must be what she had meant. But the mistake that had caused it all wasn't mine, surely? They were her mistakes – hers and Uncle Bill's.

I remembered a lesson at school when the teacher was asking about our fathers' war careers and I said that mine was out in Burma from 1943 until the end of the war in 1945.

'That can't be right,' the teacher said. 'He must have had leave during that time.' Of course, she was thinking about the fact that I was born in November 1945. But in reality, the man I grew up calling 'Dad' didn't meet me until I was six months old. It seemed Mum had been having an intense affair with Bill. Many women did have encounters, liaisons, affairs while their men were away fighting. It was a difficult time; people were afraid and lonely. These things happen. Many illegitimate children were born, and many men left their unfaithful wives when they got back from the front line. But my dad didn't. He stayed.

You would have to know my dad to understand why he did this. He was a gentle, kind man who loved my mum to distraction. He forgave his wife and understood that she had felt lonely and afraid while he was away.

The more I thought about Mum and Bill, the sicker I felt. I thought about how giggly and flirtatious she became around him, with freshly retouched lipstick and a softer, more feminine tone of voice. I thought about that kiss I had seen in the hall the night I told her that Bill had been touching me inside my panties. I thought about all the times as a child when I was sent out to play in the garden when he came round. And a horrible suspicion began to shape in my head. Had their affair really finished the day that Dad came home from war? Or did they still get together sometimes? Was that what the fight was about when I was eleven? Had Aunt Gwen found out they were still having an affair? Surely he had stopped having sex with my mother by the time he started having sex with me?

Maybe this would go some way to explain why Mum hadn't believed me when I told her that Bill was kissing and hurting me. She just couldn't believe it of someone who was my biological father, and her lover. That's why she thought I was making it up. Because she couldn't face the truth about the nasty, evil man who was her lover.

But why would she insist that I was to blame for everything that had gone wrong in the family? It seemed to me that my only 'sin' was being born – and there wasn't much I could do about that. Mum said I had ruined everyone's lives by raking up past mistakes, but they were his and her mistakes, not mine or Steves's. We were the victims in this trauma. But I felt so wretched that I took all the guilt onto myself. I believed that I must have been a really bad person, because otherwise these things that had happened wouldn't have happened to me. I had tried to be a good girl, I had asked God to protect me and help me. But I must be a bad person because God wasn't listening.

A few days after the life-shattering revelation, I had a doctor's appointment to talk about the fact that I was having very bad periods. My GP was kind to me and asked if I had any other worries, at which point I broke down. I wanted to tell him everything, wanted to pour my heart out to this health professional, who seemed to sense that something else was wrong in my life.

But I didn't. How could I explain the horrendous abuse that had been going on for the last ten years, since I was seven years old? How could I tell him of the pain, humiliation and constant belittlement I suffered at the hands of my mother? Bill had drummed it into me that I wouldn't be believed. He constantly reminded me that all the family knew how much he cared about me. How I willingly spent time with him. How I showed the world that I loved him.

Would this kind doctor have believed me? I was scared that he wouldn't. So I said I was fine, just tired after the pre-nursing course and the experiences in hospital. I told him I was still getting the headaches and period pains but that otherwise I was just OK.

He said he would change my current prescription to some new, stronger tablets that would take away the period pains and the headaches and make me feel a lot better. At that stage I would have taken anything to feel better. Clutching the prescription, I made my way to the nearest chemist, disappointed that I hadn't found the courage to tell my GP about my problems but relieved that he thought my physical complaints could be solved by taking a few pills.

We trusted our doctors back then, were in awe of them. If they said these pills were the right ones to take for our problems, then take them we did. Benzodiazepines were still seen as safe wonder drugs, although a few research studies had raised warnings about their addictive nature. Millions of people, mostly women, were prescribed them on repeat prescription for years and years on end. And I was one of these women.

As time went on, I began to feel better. The headaches almost stopped and my periods, although still very heavy, were not as painful. Apparently, any kind of stress will make menstruation more painful, so when the pills helped me to cope better with the dysfunctional family I was part of, the period pains got less.

As regards my career, I didn't have the heart to argue any more after Mum's bombshell. She contacted the college to enquire about me recommencing the nursing course. I didn't want to do this, but as far as she was concerned it wasn't up to me. However, the principal of the college had heard from the matron of the hospital where I had been working and between them they had decided that it wasn't a good idea for me to continue my nursing career at that point. The practical part, which was where I became unstuck, was a major part of the course in the second year, so they thought that maybe I should come back to nursing when I was older.

My mother was furious and was about to give the principal an earful, but the principal said that there was another opportunity I might like to try for, one that she thought would suit me better. The government had set up a pilot scheme for training medical receptionists. Only six students were going to be selected and she wondered if I would like a place on this course? Mum could see some prestige in this, a government-sponsored pilot scheme, so she said yes, I would like to accept a place.

She didn't consult me, of course. There was no question of me switching to the journalism course I had longed to do.

As it happens, I had been so happy at college that I was relieved to be going back to any course that didn't involve nursing. I went back in September 1962, still only seventeen, and embarked on the first medical receptionist training course in the country. I still saw all my good friends from the pre-nursing course and still felt very much part of the student family. This helped me to begin to come to terms with the tumultuous events of the summer months.

I didn't see Steve, my half-brother, again for a long time. He didn't come over to our house and I didn't go to see him. Although the pain was still there, college life and my youth helped me deal with it.

I continued to feel a strong sense of betrayal, though. I was used to Mum letting me down and hurting me, but this surpassed everything she had ever done in the past. And what must my dear, gentle, kind dad be feeling? We never once discussed it. He kept out of my way. I presume he meant this to protect me and not cause me any more anguish, but I could have used someone to talk to at home and there was no one there.

Uncle Bill kept away for the rest of that year. I suppose things must have been difficult for him at home. No doubt Gwen was furious with him. I thought about her and her family, and Steve in particular. You can't just turn off a love as strong as I had felt for him and I cried myself to sleep many, many times.

'Gwen and the family hate you now,' Mum told me, and I believed her. So I stayed away.

How could I have gone to see them? It was all my fault, wasn't it? If I hadn't been born, their lives would have continued just fine. No one would be hurting now.

It was my guilt, my shame, and I would have to carry it for most of the rest of my life.`

Chapter Fourteen

In contrast to my home life, I really enjoyed my time at college. I joined a theatre group, sang with a glee club and continued to be a member of the church choir, as well as singing in the band on Friday nights. Gradually I began to live the life of a normal student. I had my quiet moments, when the dark thoughts crept up on me, but I had become an expert at hiding all the horrible bits of my life and pretending that things were good.

Mum continued to be harsh and cruel. My older siblings had all left – Ellen and Rosie were married and Tom was overseas with the Marines, but Anne remained at home, where she got to take over the role of Mum's favourite, in contrast to me, the person who had ruined her life. I was too busy to spend much time at home, because on top of my social life I had to work hard to keep up with the course work, but that was all for the best.

The great thing was that I hadn't seen Bill for over a year. He had gone, and as time went by I let myself believe that was it, that I would never see him again, never have to do those despicable things with him again. I was trying very hard to put all the pain of my past where it belonged – in the past. I was trying to make another norm, one that was happy and free from fear.

When I was eighteen years old I met an actor called Alistair, who was the original tall, dark and handsome man. He was full of charisma and an amazing actor as well. All the girls adored him so I was completely bowled over when he asked me to go on a date. Me!

I was shocked and astonished but I said yes straight away (and almost added 'Yes, please!').

We started dating, but during the early months of our relationship, once again, Uncle Bill came back on the scene. I arrived home one day after college and there he was, sitting in our living room with a mug of tea in his hand. I was shocked and went straight to my room but Mum called me down to speak to him. What was she thinking? Did she think that I would start treating him as my father? Did she really think that I could have this relationship with him? I had told her about how he hurt me, so what was she thinking? I went down and said hello and made the bare minimum of polite conversation, then escaped up to my room again. Nothing was said about the revelation that he was my father, or about the end of my relationship with his son. He never brought it up, and I didn't either.

For a while after that I managed to avoid being alone with him, but he seemed almost to be stalking me until he could get me alone and try to lure me away with him.

'Bill wants to take you into town, so get your coat,' Mum said one Saturday when he had dropped in. 'It's a long time since you spent time together. I'm going out with Auntie Mary. See you both later!'

She left, and Bill looked at me with his awful, awful grin. 'Come on, Cassie, we can have fun. We could buy you some new shoes or something.'

'I'm not coming out with you!' I said firmly.

'Your mum said you've got to come. Do you want to take it up with her? She'll be very cross with you.'

'I'm not coming with you any more,' I insisted. 'You can't make me. If you try to force me, I'll tell Alistair.' I just said this because it was the first thing that came into my head. I hadn't really thought it through.

Uncle Bill laughed. 'What would he think of you if you told him? He'll say, if you didn't like what was going on, why didn't you stop it? Why didn't you tell someone before?'

I could see how it might look to an outsider. I *had* told some-one, but I hadn't been believed. What if Alistair thought I had wanted to have sex with the man I now knew to be my own father? Surely he would run a mile?

Bill threatened that if I didn't agree to have sex with him he would tell Alistair about our relationship, tell him that I had instigated it, that I was the one who made things sexual. I was horrified! Horrified that he could do this and horrified at the thought that he might be believed.

Would he really tell? I didn't understand the law at that age. I thought that it would be seen as my fault because I hadn't done anything to stop it. I was scared of losing Alistair, with whom I was completely infatuated. I was too naïve to realise that I had any choice in the matter, even at the age of eighteen. When I was younger and I had told Mum about Bill abusing me, she hadn't believed me. I had tried to put it behind me during the time Bill wasn't on the scene, but now he was back all the fears and doubts overwhelmed me again. I couldn't tell now, could I? What would I say? He had continually raped and abused me for years and years. Wouldn't people think it was strange that I hadn't told anyone before? Would they believe him? As far as I could see, I had to keep quiet – and I couldn't let him tell either. I was confused, and scared of Uncle Bill, and so I gave in and let him have his way again.

We went to the houseboat that afternoon. And the abuse continued.

During that summer of 1964, Mum hired a friend of hers, a man called Phil, to paint our kitchen. I think he was out of work and she was helping him out. Anne and my parents were going away for the day and Mum suggested that he make a start while they were out, adding that I would be at home to bring him cups of tea when he wanted them.

I didn't particularly like Phil but had no reason to fear him. After everyone left, I began to clear the breakfast dishes and put them in the sink. Suddenly he came up behind me and grabbed me around the waist.

I went rigid, I was so shocked, then I managed to spin round and push him away.

He laughed and made a joke about it, then carried on with his painting.

I tried to dismiss the incident but my past experiences came into my head and I began to feel nervous. After clearing the dishes, I walked into the hallway to go up to my room and keep out of his way. But I never got that far.

Again Phil grabbed me, lunging and trying to kiss my face. I screamed at him to stop.

'Come on, it's fun. You know it is,' he laughed, thrusting his hand up my skirt and tugging at my panties.

Not again. Why was this happening to me? Why me?

'Get away from me! Stop it!' I yelled, and I struggled with all of my strength. He pushed his hot, now sweaty body against me and I began to cry, feeling his penis hardening against my stomach.

His face was distorted as he rubbed his body up and down against me, arousing himself. And then came the words that made the whole ugly episode even more despicable. 'I'm allowed to do anything to you. He said I could. You know you like it, so stop playing games and let's get on with it. He said you would pretend to dislike this but I know different and I can do what I want.'

I couldn't believe my ears. Could it be true? Had Bill really given permission for this man to abuse his own biological daughter? How sick was that?

'Get away!' I screamed. 'Get away from me! I hate you! Stop this!' I pushed and pushed at him, praying with all my heart that he would stop. Then my prayers were answered. Someone knocked on the front door. Phil jumped, I pushed past him and ran to the door and flung it open then stepped out onto the doorstep.

It was the milkman, come for his money. I was never so happy to see anyone in my whole life. The milkman realised that something wasn't quite right.

'Are you OK, love?' he asked, looking at my ruffled clothes and flushed face.

I started to say, 'No, I'm not.' At that point, Phil walked out past us and said everything was fine, he was just leaving. He hurried off down the street.

After the milkman had gone I shut the door and locked it, still shaking, still shocked. Nothing had happened really. Certainly nothing as nasty as all the other abuse I had suffered. But even though Phil hadn't actually been able to rape me, I still felt terrified. Was I not safe from other men? Was this what all men wanted from me?

I had finished with boyfriends in the past because sex was the only thing on their minds. Alistair had said he respected me and wanted to wait, and that was one of the reasons I trusted him and liked being with him. Suddenly I felt a strong need to see him. I washed myself thoroughly, dressed and locked up the house and went over to his place.

As soon as Alistair looked at me, he knew there was something very wrong. I didn't mean to tell him but I couldn't help it. I was still shaking with a mixture of fear and indignation. I told him about how Phil had tried to assault me. I told him everything. Except that I didn't tell him Bill had said it would be OK. How could I tell him that? How could I tell him that my father had given Phil permission to sexually abuse me, abuse me in the way he himself had been doing for virtually all of my life?

Before I could argue, Alistair put me in a taxi and the two of us headed back to my house, where he wanted me to tell Mum everything. To say I was terrified was an understatement. I'd told her once before about Bill, and look how that had turned out!

But Mum approved of Alistair. He was from a very wealthy family, a family that was respected in the community. An upper-class family. So he was OK in my mother's book. This time I seemed to have got it right. Alistair was also charming and good-looking and he knew how to handle Mum.

When the family came home, we asked to talk to my parents in private. Mum insisted that Dad take my younger sister out to buy sweets at the shop down the road and we went into the best room.

It wasn't easy telling her, because Phil was a friend of hers, but tell her I did. With the exception of the missing bits.

Alistair was so angry, he said he wanted to kill this man.

My mother realised she should probably be playing the concerned parent at this point so she stood up and came over to me. 'No one,' she said sternly, 'no one will hurt my daughter and not pay for it.'

I was stunned. This was a new one! Where did that come from?

'I just want to forget all about it and pretend it never happened,' I said, scared of what else might come out. 'As long as he doesn't come to the house or come near me again, I'll be fine.'

But no. This woman who suddenly cared for her daughter picked up the phone to call the police. I was absolutely stunned!

Was this the same woman who had called me names when I'd confided in her about the darkest, most horrific secret of my young life?

The same woman I had witnessed kissing my abuser and telling him that she hadn't believed a word I'd said?

What I didn't know at the time was that Mum had been having an affair with Phil but straight after leaving our house earlier that day he had phoned her to call a halt to it. So she was already angry with him. I had given her the opportunity to hurt him in a very serious way. How dare he spurn her? He would pay dearly for that.

Despite my attempts to prevent it going any further, the police arrived. They were very kind. A policewoman with bright red hair asked to speak to me in another room. She started by telling me that if a man did anything to a girl or a young woman that they didn't want, then it was an offence. She went on to say that if I had been younger then it would have been an even more serious offence. I began to cry. She comforted me and said that I was to take my time, I could tell her anything and she would endeavour to put the offender behind bars.

She thought my tears were about the afternoon's events. Little did she know.

My tears were for the girl who hadn't known any of that, who hadn't dared to tell anyone what a man was doing to her.

I explained what had happened with Phil and she wrote everything down. I was then examined in the best room of the house. All the time the policewoman comforted and reassured me that she would make sure justice was done. She said she would also talk to the milkman who had saved me that day so he could be a witness.

She was so kind that I wanted to spill everything out. Wanted to tell her that actually this was nothing compared to the abuse I'd been suffering over the last eighteen years. *He* hadn't actually touched me intimately. *He* hadn't raped me. I wanted to tell. But I couldn't do it. And then my chance was gone.

The next few weeks felt like a dream, as if I was living some-one else's life. The house was the same. The family were the same. The dog was the same. But Mum wasn't. She wasn't the same. Gone were the jibes. Gone were the unkind remarks and the ridicule. She was actually kind to me. She talked to me as if she cared about me. She spoke quietly to me, which was unheard of in our house.

I tried to like it. I tried to believe in it and enjoy it. Wasn't this what I had always wanted? I tried to believe this was how it would be from now on. But I couldn't. I was a master at pretending so I could always spot it in other people. I knew this wouldn't last. I knew it wasn't real.

I didn't have long to wait. Phil was taken to court the follow-ing week. It was a horrible experience for me. I was cross-examined by his defence barrister, who insinuated that I had asked for it. He made it sound as though I had flirted with this man and enjoyed the attention and the kissing. I was horrified. I tried to defend myself but was stopped. I didn't understand the way courts work. Why should I have? This was my first encounter.

The court heard from the milkman, my mother and my boyfriend. When Alistair spoke, the court fell silent. After all, he was good with an audience and had practised what he was going to say, as if it was a script in a play. It was all true, but he put it across very well.

After two days, the judge found Phil guilty of attempted sexual assault and actual assault. It was then disclosed that he had been cautioned for several sexual assaults before, mostly with young girls.

As we left the courts I will never forget the look on his wife's face. She obviously didn't believe my story and thought her husband was innocent. I felt awful, particularly when I noticed she was pregnant. The court only gave Phil a two-year suspended sentence in view of his wife's pregnancy. I heard on the grapevine a few years later that his teenage daughter had given birth to twins and that he was the father. He really was a thoroughly nasty individual.

It took a long time for me to recover from the court case and the feelings of guilt about Phil's wife and family. Uncle Bill stayed away throughout this time, possibly afraid that he would be implicated. After all, he had given his permission for the assault to take place, hadn't he? He had told Phil that it was OK to sexually abuse me, his own daughter. So he had to stay away, didn't he?

It was nice that his abuse had ceased for the time being. But it didn't take long for Mum to get over her fake concern for me and revert to her normal behaviour. She couldn't manage to be nice to me for long.

Chapter Fifteen

At the time of the court case, Alistair and I had just got engaged. Mum was delighted at the thought of me marrying into the 'upper classes' and whenever my fiancé was around she became the loving mother who wanted nothing but the best for her daughter. Life had been looking up. But after the case everything seemed to have changed – both in her behaviour and in his.

One day, when I arrived at Alistair's place to spend the weekend, I noticed that my usual bed in the spare room hadn't been made up. When I asked where I was to sleep, my charming fiancé said, 'In with me.'

'But I thought we were waiting until we got married,' I protested. 'I thought we had agreed about that.'

'We're getting married, so what's the harm?' he said with a smile. 'There are no other beds made up, love, so you have no choice.'

Suddenly I saw him as just the same as Uncle Bill and Phil. All they seemed to want me for was sex. To play their games, to satisfy their needs. I was upset but more angry than anything. He knew what the court case had done to me; he knew how I felt about sex. He didn't know the reason, because I didn't tell him – I didn't tell anyone except Mum – but he knew all the same.

I couldn't get home that night as Alistair didn't have a car and we weren't on a bus route, plus it was too far to walk. But I did have a choice. I had gone into the bathroom and was worried that since he had changed his attitude about waiting for marriage, he might try and force me to have sex with him that night. I began to get washed and ready for bed but I didn't want to go out onto the landing in my nightie just in case he leapt on me. I couldn't decide what to do and I felt too nervous to talk to Alistair about it, so in the end I just slept in the bath, using towels as a pillow and covers.

The next day, after a brief conversation, I broke off my engagement. I was disappointed in Alistair because I had thought he was different. I thought he was interested in me and not just in having sex with me, but it seems that wasn't the case. He pointed out that it was 1964 and most girls slept with their fiancés – but I wasn't most girls. I was me, not a sexual plaything.

When I went home and told Mum, she was incandescent with rage, all her plans for moving into the upper classes through my marriage smashed to smithereens. She didn't speak to me for a long time after that. But that was nothing new.

Over the next few months I dated several boyfriends but it seemed they all wanted only one thing from me and I began to believe that this was all I was worth. They sometimes became very angry when I wouldn't do as they wanted but I held my ground. I began to wonder if I had 'sexual plaything' tattooed on my forehead because that's certainly how it seemed. I liked some of them but they never stayed around when they realised there wasn't going to be any sex.

Then I had some wonderful news. Claire, my best friend from primary school, was to be married and I was to be chief bridesmaid. We hadn't seen each other very much throughout our teens and, what with college and singing, the rest of my life had been filled with Bill or family chores. Claire had taken a job in a shop when she left school at fifteen and had met her future husband when she was seventeen. We had met up a few times, and we were both bridesmaids when my sister Ellen got married, but since then we hadn't seen each other very much. I was over the moon when she asked me to be her chief brides-maid, something that we had talked about as children. Planning the wedding meant I was back with my second family, feeling safe and loved.

The ceremony was lovely. I wore a glorious yellow organza and silk gown and felt like a princess as we drove round the town in the best man's open-topped car. It was an unbelievably happy day, and although it was my best friend's wedding day and not mine I didn't think she could possibly be as happy as I was.

Mum was working in a café nearby and after the wedding reception I popped in to see her, still dressed in my yellow bridesmaid's dress. Mum was friendly with the landlady of the pub next door, who was called Dottie, and her son Edward happened to be in the café when I walked in so we chatted for a while.

'Edward thinks you're really attractive,' Mum said to me later. 'You should pop in and see him at the pub some time.'

Was my mother matchmaking? Paying me compliments? Wonders would never cease. I called in at the pub the next day and got talking to Edward, who turned out to be a very gentle man with a lovely sense of humour. He asked me out on a date and I accepted.

At this stage I was working as a receptionist for a group medical practice in a nearby city, a job I loved. The doctors treated me well and became almost like friends to me. One of my duties was to write the repeat prescriptions for patients, and it was only while doing this that I realised for the first time that the pills I was taking were actually antidepressants. I mentioned it to one of the doctors and he was horrified when I told him the dose of medication I was taking and the length of time I had been taking it. I tried to stop taking them but the headaches they had been prescribed to treat came back worse than ever so, after a chat with my GP, I decided to keep taking them. No one mentioned anything to me about dependency or long-term side effects. If the GP thought it was OK, surely it was?

Things continued to go well between Edward and me. He asked if I would sleep with him but when I said no he respected that and didn't push me. And then, after we had been seeing each other for a few months, he asked me to marry him. I knew little about love and marriage at that stage. He made me feel happy and he made me feel safe, so I said yes, I'd love to. I would be part of a loving family and the wife of a man who loved me for myself. It sounded perfect.

We planned to have an engagement party, and because Edward's parents ran a pub and it was difficult for them to take a night off we decided to have it there. Logical decision, you would think – but someone was not pleased.

'He's the son of a publican!' Mum exclaimed, as though this was an almighty sin. 'A party in a pub! What do you take me for? I'm not going to any party in a common public house!'

I tried to remind her that he had been living in a pub when she pushed me to go round and visit him that first day but she wasn't having it. If my engagement party was held in a pub, she wasn't going to be there.

We went ahead and had the party anyway, but none of my family came. Mum made sure of that.

'You've made me ill over all of this,' she shouted. 'You must be trying very hard to hurt me. Well, you've succeeded.'

I was still confused. 'But I'm so happy with him, happier than I have been for a long time,' I said, but this made her even more angry. Suddenly she threw herself on the floor, clutching her chest.

Was it another game? Was she play-acting to scare me? She succeeded.

Anne started screaming, 'She's ill, you're making her ill!'

I called the doctor. Our GP came and examined her and after one of the shortest examinations I've ever heard of he pronounced her fit and well.

'She's fine, Cassie,' he said as he left. 'Nothing at all wrong with her.'

I never got angry, but I was angry now. I marched into the front room.

'The doctor said you're fine, that there's nothing wrong with you,' I told her.

She jumped up and started raining blows on me. I ran into the hall and she came after me, grabbing me by the hair and knocking me against the banisters. As I pushed her away, she pulled a hank of hair out of my head. I reeled back in pain. Whatever happened to being ill?

Then Mum ran upstairs to my room and started throwing my belongings down the stairs, where my young sister proceeded to hurl them out into the garden.

'I'll show you!' Mum screamed. 'I'll show you. You get out of here and don't come back. All you've ever done is cause me pain and hurt. You can have what I let you take but nothing that I paid for!' She sounded furious and hateful.

'Mum, please don't. I was relieved the doctor said you were OK. Please stop this,' I begged, but she didn't listen.

She was throwing me out. It was midnight by this stage. How could she do this? Where would I go? What could I do?

I was pushed outside and the door was slammed shut. I stood with all my belongings on the lawn in front of the family home. It was very dark and very cold. And once again I was alone.

The only person I could turn to was my fiancé.

Fortunately Dottie, his mother, agreed to take me in. The next day she went round to try and talk sense into my mother but she came back seething with rage, saying that Mum hadn't listened to a word. She didn't agree with the engagement but had no good reason to give. She wouldn't have me in the house if I continued to see Edward. She would definitely play no part in any wedding arrangements.

Dottie was furious. She made up her spare room with floral curtains and bedding and told me it was mine and that I was welcome to stay there until I married her son. I was so touched that I began to cry. This lady, this wonderful caring woman who was to be my mum-in-law, came straight over and put her arms around me.

'It's good to have you here,' she said. 'I already see you as part of the family.'

Is this what mothers do? I wondered. Is this the kind of love I have been missing all my life? I was overjoyed. This is what I had always wanted, to be part of a loving family. A family like Claire's. A family where I was loved and safe. The only things I missed from my old life were my beloved dad and my best friend, my dog Bobby. Unbeknown to me, Dottie went to see Mum again and asked if I could have my dog. The reply was that as far as Mum was concerned I had no dog. I was heartbroken, but not surprised. I'd been on the receiving end of this kind of cruelty many times before.

I had to let this go. I missed Dad a lot and was often tempted to ring him but I knew that if Mum answered, his life wouldn't have been worth living.

The huge bonus in the whole situation was that I wouldn't have to see Bill any more. He couldn't get to me now that I was living with Dottie and Edward. There was always someone around to stop him. So I really was safe from the evil, nasty man and his despicable acts.

Back in the 1960s you needed your parents' consent to marry if you were under twenty-one. Edward and I wrote to Mum and she refused point blank to give it, so we had no alternative but to wait until my twenty-first birthday on 12 November 1966. I wanted my dad to give me away but Mum had already said that he had 'no right' and that she wouldn't allow him to do this for me. She and I knew who she thought should.

Even if Bill hadn't abused me, even if I had discovered the truth about my parentage and things had been good between him and me, I would still have wanted the dad who brought me up to give me away. As it was, I asked my brother Tom.

Mum wasn't finished yet. She rang the vicar of the church in which I was to be married and claimed that because I was under twenty-one he couldn't call the banns in church. Our vicar told us that he had assured her that as long as I would be twenty-one on the day of the wedding he had the right to read the banns and plan the service. He said he had never, in thirty years of working for the church, had this kind of issue. He went on to tell us that he had to put the phone down on Mum to put a stop to the torrent of the abuse she directed at him. I could only imagine her anger and was secretly quite worried about what her next move would be. Because there would be another move. I knew there would.

On the Friday before my big day I received a package. In my hurry to get to work I took all my post and this package with me to open on the way. I didn't recognise the writing on the envelope and couldn't think what it was. I was actually on the ferry with a friend when I opened it and suddenly the deck and my lap were covered with tiny bits of paper. When I bent to pick up some of the pieces, I realised what the contents were. I recognised some of the special paper on which I had written poems for my mother when I was a small child, hoping against hope that they would make her love me. It seems she had kept every poem I had written, every certificate I had won and every story that was mine. Now she had torn all these items to shreds and posted them to me, just before my wedding. The cruelty of the gesture stunned me, even though I was used to her by now. It could only have been done to hurt me. She wanted to spoil my happiness on the big day.

'Try not to think about it,' my friend said angrily. 'It's her problem. This just shows what she can be like. Try and forget it happened.'

I gathered all the pieces back into the package and continued with my day and did my best to push her out of my mind, but it wasn't easy after a stunt like that.

On the morning of my wedding I woke up with no voice. I couldn't say a word. I know now that I was suffering from severe stress, but at the time I just thought I was coming down with a cold or something. The reality was that, although I didn't show my new family or my friends, I was overcome with worry about what the day might bring, and above all I was getting increasingly anxious about my wedding night. My fiancé had been patient and I thought, naïvely, that when I was married everything would be OK. That magically sex would become wonderful, that it would come easily to me. Married to someone who loved me – how could it not be good? How could I not want to make love to this lovely man, my husband?

It couldn't have rained any more that day if I had paid for rain. The heavens opened, and some of Edward's friends, who were firemen, tried to shelter me under huge umbrellas as I ran up the church path. I descended into the church lobby with my dress hitched up around my waist. What a sight I must have been!

At the altar I had to mime my vows, making a promise to go back into the vicarage on my return from honeymoon to repeat them audibly. I kept glancing over my shoulder in the church, hoping against hope that Mum would turn up at the last minute – just as I had watched for her years before when I was three years old and dancing in a concert. But of course she didn't. Hope disappointed me once more.

But Edward and I were married, and at last I was pretty sure I was safe. Safe from Mum, and safe from Uncle Bill.

Chapter Sixteen

Such a little word, 'safe'. A little word with a huge meaning for me. Married life was going to be safe, or so I thought. But on the first night of our marriage I realised that there are many different forms of unsafe. I stupidly thought that once I was married that ugly word 'sex' would change into a wonderful word, meaning something else. 'Love' perhaps. Something that it had never meant to me before. But a band of gold on my finger and some vows spoken in a church were not enough to overcome a lifetime of conditioning.

On our wedding night my kind and patient husband tried to show his love and tried to make love to me, but it ended with me screaming and sobbing. I became hysterical and this poor man didn't know how to cope with me. He soothed me, saying that we would be OK and that over time our lovemaking would become something special.

I must have appeared frigid, unloving and cold. I must have seemed hysterical to this lovely man who had no idea of my demons or the chaos in my head. How could he? I'd never told him. I'd never told anyone – except Mum.

After our honeymoon, life settled down. I loved having my little house and garden. I was a good housewife, as I had lots of experience of doing chores. But this was different. This was mine. My own home. My husband didn't push the sex issue but I was aware of his growing impatience. We had a good social life, and often had Edward's friends around for card evenings and suppers. Life was fine.

Then, one day, my new safety was shattered. My husband had gone to work and I had a day off. There was a knock on my door and I went to open it, not ready for what I was to find standing on my doorstep.

Him. Uncle Bill. For a moment my heart stopped. I began to tremble. All the fears of the past came flooding back. I was straight back to being the child again. I had frozen to the spot. He just walked past me into my hallway and the sickly grimace on his face made my tummy churn. What was he doing here? Why had he come?

What a stupid, stupid question. We both knew why he had come. I guessed that Mum must have given him my address.

At first he just looked around. He said how nice I had made the place. He seemed quite calm. Almost normal, whatever that meant. But then suddenly he made a grab for me. I pushed him away and ran to the back of the house, heading for the garden, but he was too fast. He grabbed me and held me tightly.

'I've missed you, Cassie,' he leered. 'I've missed all our fun games.'

'I'm a married woman now,' I cried. 'You can't do this to me any more,' hoping that this would make him leave me alone. But it made him laugh.

'Yes, I know. That makes it even better.' I didn't understand. 'Now we can go back to our adult games as you're living a married life. It'll be OK,' he said, grinning.

Living a married life? Little did he know that all the horrendous times he had abused me and made me take part in his evil games, all of this had rendered me incapable of living a normal married life. My new husband and I had never consummated our marriage. Every time Edward got too close, too intimate, I went cold and pushed him away. I often became hysterical and he would retreat and apologise, saying he wouldn't push me. Then we would become distant and I would be full of shame and guilt. This guilt was different from the guilt I'd felt as a child. But how could he have understood this? He didn't know, did he? I didn't tell him. I didn't tell anyone.

He tried to kiss me. 'Come on, let's have some fun,' he said. I pushed him away.

'I'll scream!' I threatened, but this seemed to make him more excited.

He pulled me down onto the hall floor and I struggled, oh how I struggled. He was writhing around on top of me, trying to get a hand inside my trousers, when he must have heard something. Suddenly he jumped up and away from me, swearing. I scrambled to my feet and decided that I would stand my ground. I couldn't go on like this. He couldn't hurt me any more.

'I'll tell,' I said. 'I'll tell my husband.'

This made him laugh again. 'And how could you do that? What would you say?' He seemed highly amused. 'How will you explain, when I say that we have been doing this for years? He won't believe you. No one would. If you hadn't liked the games then why didn't you tell someone in the beginning?'

He knew I had. But I hadn't been believed.

Then I had a brainwave. 'I'll cry rape!' I told him. 'I'll scream and cry rape. I'll call the police and make a formal complaint.' He seemed surprised that I was standing up to him. 'Even if I am only believed for this one time, it will be worth it!'

This seemed to stop him in his tracks. He knew I'd taken a man to court before. I took it all the way. He didn't know that prosecuting Phil had been my mother's doing. I had never seen him look so worried. I hoped and prayed that this would make him go away forever. That at last it would end. At last I really would be safe.

But after a few minutes he said, 'If I am accused of rape I'll tell everyone that we had a relationship and this time I only came round here to end it.' He seemed to be thinking on his feet. 'Yeah, that's what I'll say. I was trying to end it and just to get your own back on me you cried rape!' He was grinning. 'Anyway, how many people would believe you, if you now say it had happened again with someone else after you've already accused Phil?' He was really pleased with himself.

I was scared. Would people doubt what had happened with Phil if I now accused Bill? What would everyone think? What would my husband think?

I did tell, I did

I was shattered. He had won again.

'I'll go now,' he said, 'but I'll be back and the games will start again. Have no doubt about that!'

He left me feeling absolutely destroyed. I knew he couldn't use the defence that we'd had a relationship, because then he could be prosecuted for incest. But what if people just plain didn't believe me? They might think I was a hysteric who accuses men of rape after hardly any provocation. And did I really want Edward to know about all this? Did I want him to know about all my guilt and shame?

I became very stressed about the situation, and that made it even more difficult for Edward and me to try and have a normal sex life. One evening, after talking about it at length, we decided that I would go to the GP and ask for a referral to a psychiatrist who worked with sexual issues. I agreed in the hope that it would improve my marriage. I really wanted things to get better, with all my heart.

On the day of my appointment with the psychiatrist, Dottie came with me, as Edward was working and I'd been told I had to have someone to look after me after the session. I saw the consultant for about five minutes and he explained that they were going to use a technique called abreactive psychotherapy. You would have thought I would have asked what this meant but I didn't. I trusted that whatever it was, it was going to help me lose my fear of sex and make my marriage work.

I was taken into a small room and told to lie on a couch, then the doctor injected something into my arm. After what I thought was a few minutes, but was actually about an hour, I awoke to find a nurse offering me a cup of tea. And then I was sent home.

This went on every Tuesday for six months. On the evenings after the therapy I used to feel great. Relaxed and happy. It was after one of these sessions that Edward and I finally managed to make love. I didn't enjoy it, but it wasn't horrendous. He was kind and gentle and made me feel loved throughout.

After about five months of treatments, I asked to see the consultant to find out more about the injection I was being given. He explained that it was like a truth pill. He would ask me questions about my worries and I would offload them onto him. I was terrified. Had I told him? Did he know? How much had I said?

I quizzed him about what I had said but the only thing he revealed was that it was evident that I missed my dog.

If I *had* told, what would have happened? Would they have believed me? Would they want to know who my abuser was? Surely I must have mentioned the abuse and the fear of Uncle Bill? I must have done.

But nothing changed; I felt the same as I had always felt. Sex was still a dirty word. A few days after my last visit to the psychiatric unit, one morning I felt a bit strange. Not sick, just strange. My period was late. It couldn't be, could it? It had only happened once, so how could I be? But I knew I was. I knew I was pregnant.

I was overjoyed. That one time when I had managed to have sex with my husband had brought about this wonderful new

I did tell, I did

life inside of me. We had never spoken about babies. Because of the sexual problems, I suppose it wasn't relevant. I didn't know how Edward felt about a family. I didn't know how he felt about babies and being a dad. But I knew I was having his baby and I was over the moon.

I didn't tell him straight away. I wanted to be sure so I went to the GP, and when the test eventually came back positive I was crying with joy. My own baby. My own real-life china doll. My child.

I told Edward that evening, but instead of being thrilled he was confused. He didn't understand how it had happened. We had only made love once. He wasn't sure how he felt, as he knew nothing about babies and had certainly not thought of having one. He wasn't unkind or angry. He wasn't being nasty or trying to hurt me. He was just shocked. But however he meant it to come across, I was mortified. Suddenly the joy of knowing I was to be a mother had taken a severe downturn. I tried to reassure him that nothing would change, that we would be OK. He was a good man but he just wasn't quite ready for the commitment of having a child.

Dottie, on the other hand, was overjoyed. My pregnancy was wonderful, my hair and skin looked great and I was very healthy throughout. I couldn't wait to be a mum. Only one thing stood in the way of true happiness and that was the fear of Uncle Bill returning. Not only was I afraid for myself, but I was also desperately scared for the child I was carrying. Would he ever try to hurt my child? Would he claim him or her as a grandchild?

Then one day, when I was about three months pregnant, I got a phone call at work and I was astonished to hear Mum's voice on the line. What's more, she was crying.

'It's Bill,' she sobbed. 'He's had a stroke and he's in a coma. You must go and see him,' she pleaded. 'I can't, can I? What would people think?'

Go and see him? Was she mad? And then she began to declare her love for this man, the man who was my father, the man who had abused me for the whole of my life. The evil, nasty man with whom she had continued to have an affair for over twenty years, ever since the war.

'I love him, you know I do. I always have. You must go and see him for me and give him my love. Comfort him.'

I didn't speak. I couldn't speak. What could I say?

Could I have told her that at last I could see an end to my pain and fear?

Could I have told her that I was happy? Happy that the games, the toys would soon be a thing of the past.

Should I have told her that I wasn't sad, because his death would protect me, would stop it all?

Should I have said all of this?

Probably I should have, but I didn't. I didn't, because the pretence that had protected him and her for all the years of my past, that pretence would stop me from saying any of these things. The people who knew us, who thought that I loved this evil man, would expect me to visit him. They would expect to see me crying and heartbroken. They would expect me to be at his side.

I did tell, I did

'Yes, I'll go,' I said with a heavy heart. 'I'll give him your love.'

And so I went to see him.

He was lying in a side room, on his own. The doctor asked if I was a relative. I couldn't say I was his daughter – in my heart he had never been my father – so I told him I was his goddaughter. A while after I arrived, a nurse came in and looked pleased that I was there. She reached under his pillow and brought out a small photograph of me. I was shocked. I recognised the picture. It was one I'd had taken for college a few years before. Mum must have given it to him. Apparently they asked his wife, Gwen, if he had a daughter. When Gwen said no, they changed the subject. Some of the staff thought that perhaps I was a girlfriend, a younger, much younger girl-friend, so they'd hoped I would visit him.

I explained who I was and said there had been a family rift and that I didn't want his wife to know I had been to see him. Even on his deathbed I was protecting him. Or was I? I like to think I was protecting her.

Over the years, after learning more about men like him, I often shuddered at the thought that perhaps he used to look at my picture and pleasure himself. But I had to stop these thoughts and tell myself that I don't know he did this. I didn't know, I only wondered. Wasn't it bad enough to know and live with what he *had* done?

I sat by his bed and he looked so small. So frail. So bad, so evil, so nasty. Illness had not changed who he was. I cried, and the tears were seen as tears of grief for this man they thought

I loved. I suppose I was grieving in a way. But not for him or his impending death. I was grieving for my childhood and the innocence that he had stolen from me when I was just a little girl. I cried a lot that day, but mostly tears of relief.

As I cried over him, I was careful not to touch him. I didn't ever want to feel that touch again. I cried for the little girl that was me. His lying in this hospital bed, waiting for death, hadn't changed any of that. Dying hadn't made him good. Only death would make it stop. It was then that I decided to tell him.

I had been told during my brief nursing training that even in a coma a patient could hear. This was the last sense to go. So I told him.

I told him how he had ruined my life, how he had taken away my childhood and made me live in fear and horror for most of my life. I told him how I hated what he had done to me and that I would never, never forgive him. I know that we are told we should forgive. I know that as a Christian I should have been able to say it was all OK, that I forgave him for everything he ever did to me.

But I couldn't. I couldn't because I didn't.

I said that the one thing that he would ever do for me that I could thank him for was to die. Wicked? Unchristian? Unforgivable of me? Yes, but honest.

Then as I stood up to leave this cold hospital room, my tears stopped and I allowed myself to feel the relief. It was almost over. I was to be truly safe. But more importantly, so was my unborn child. He would never hurt me again and he would never be able to hurt my son or daughter. All it would take was one phone call, the call that would tell me that my prayers had been answered.

The following day the call came. He had gone. God had been listening. I was safe.

Chapter Seventeen

The pregnancy went without a hitch, even though I had to stop taking my antidepressants for the duration. I really blossomed and this wonderful time was the best in my life up to this point. Not only was I to become a mum, but the evil that was Bill was dead. Literally. Dead. For the first time in my whole life, I felt free. I no longer had to look round corners or be afraid to open my front door. He really was gone. It was over.

The labour wasn't as straightforward as the pregnancy, though. My waters broke at 6.30 a.m. on a Saturday morning and it was 2.10 p.m. on the Monday when the baby was finally born by forceps delivery. So no picnic! On being asked by a nurse what I wanted to call the baby, I insisted that he was to be called Mark. I'd been convinced it was a boy, but the midwife laughed and suggested I might like to rethink this as 'Mark' was a healthy baby girl.

'Melissa,' I whispered. 'We'll call her Melissa.'

I needed surgery for repairs from the delivery, and I came round the following morning to find my mother at my bedside. She had been crying. Again, I was confused. Why was she there? What did she want?

'Oh Cassie, my lovely Cassie,' she cried.

I looked around. Was she referring to me?

'I've been so worried, you must have had an awful time,' came the words from her mouth, the words that sounded concerned and caring. 'It's over now. You just have to get well and I'll help as much as I can. You know that, don't you?'

Then I noticed that the ward sister was nearby, watching this woman at the side of my bed with kindness and respect, and it all made sense. Mum had an audience.

My voice was very croaky from the anaesthetic. 'I'm fine. Have you seen my baby? Is she OK?'

'I wasn't concerned about the baby, I was so worried about you. But I'll go and see her now,' my mother said, sounding for all the world like a natural, caring parent.

Don't be fooled, I thought. She isn't natural or caring. I *hoped* she had changed. Maybe the baby would bring us together. Hope was alive and well.

After taking my beautiful baby daughter home, I was still quite unwell and my husband did his best to look after us. Dottie also helped as much as she could, but without an audience my own mother was conspicuous by her absence. My sisters Ellen and Rosie had both had sons by this time and Tom also had a baby boy, whom my mother adored. She spent a lot of time fussing over these grandchildren, but my child couldn't expect the same treatment. Mum had shown up at the hospital after Melissa's birth because the world would expect her to come and see her new grandchild, but having done her 'duty' she had no more interest in us. Hope was dashed yet again. But life settled down and I loved every minute of being a mum.

Sadly, as time went on, Edward and I grew further and further apart. I tried to make it work but knew in my heart that I didn't love him enough – or at least, I never loved him in the right way. We had no sex life at all because I still couldn't make love. I had tried to be a good wife, tried to let him make love to me, but I couldn't. It always ended with me hysterical and in tears. I tried to escape the thoughts and images in my head but they were too strong. Every time he touched me, I froze. It felt dirty. Evil and nasty. I wanted it to stop.

Of course it wasn't evil, nasty or dirty, but that's how it felt to me. Edward didn't understand. How could he? He didn't know because I never told him. Never told him of my childhood traumas at the hands of the man who turned out to be my father. The legacy of the abuse I had suffered was very much still there. It haunted me and still had the power to ruin my life. The evil that was Bill was dead but the feelings and the memories were still very much alive.

A year after Melissa's birth, Edward and I decided to part. This kind man who loved me was the first casualty of my legacy of abuse. My GP had advised me to start taking antidepressants again after Melissa's birth when I confided in him that my marriage was in trouble – just to help me deal with the stress, he said. I trusted in his knowledge, without fear of what might be happening to me. Then the headaches were back and my medication was increased. The GP told me the pills were safe to take longterm and I believed him.

Life was tough in one way, but oh so good in others. My time with Melissa, my precious daughter, was wonderful. She only had to put her arms around my neck and everything else paled into insignificance. I didn't have much money but I managed. I took an evening job to help pay bills, working at a local pub where I knew the landlady while a neighbour looked after Melissa.

One evening a man called Larry walked me home from work, and when he asked me out for a drink I accepted. We saw each other for about six months and then, one evening after going to a dinner dance and having a few drinks, we made love. My biggest surprise was that I could make love. No problems, no hysteria. I suppose it was the alcohol. I couldn't make love with my husband, a man who loved me, so why should I have imagined I could do it with anyone else? Because of this, I wasn't taking any precautions, so I went straight off to see my GP the next morning. I had the sense to realise that if it happened once it was likely to happen again, so I was put on the Pill.

I enjoyed Larry's company. We went dancing and socialised in a way I hadn't experienced before. He was seventeen years older and seemed proud to have me on his arm. Then it happened. It couldn't be. I couldn't be. Could I?

Just before Christmas 1970 I was sick one morning, and when I realised that my period was late I got scared. Could I be pregnant? From one act of sex? Of course I could. I had only made love properly on one occasion with my husband and I became pregnant. Now, two and a bit years later, I had sex for a second time and got pregnant again. I asked Larry to come round that evening, unsure how he would take the news.

'How could you let this happen?' he demanded furiously, as if I had done 'this' on purpose. 'How could you be so stupid?' He ranted on for a while and then growled, 'You can't have it. I won't let you. You'll have to see your GP and ask for a termination.'

He reminded me of someone, the way he growled at me, the expression on his face. He reminded me of someone I didn't want to remember. I was scared at that point, seeing the nasty and evil side of him, just as there had been in Bill.

He was asking me to get rid of a baby, our baby. I tried to say that I couldn't even think of taking a baby's life. I tried to say that it would be OK and that I would look after this baby on my own. But I couldn't. I couldn't say anything. I was in shock. So I couldn't speak, and he left.

I hoped that after having a night to think things through, Larry would come round to being OK with the situation. OK with us having this child and bringing it up together. I prayed that I could keep my unborn baby, prayed that everything would come right. But hoping and praying had never been enough in my life. Once again God wasn't listening.

During the following days I heard nothing from Larry, then after about a week he arrived at my door saying he was taking me to see a doctor who could authorise my having a termination on the National Health.

I did tell, I did

I went along to see the doctor with him but everything that was said made me realise more strongly that I couldn't do it. It was against everything I believed in. I wanted to have this baby. On the way home I told Larry what I had decided.

'I can't do it, can't have a termination. It wouldn't be right.'

His face contorted and went scarlet. 'Right for who?' he growled. 'It wouldn't be right for anyone if you had a baby who had no father!'

'But it would have a father and a mother. It would have us.' I was sobbing. 'It would be loved.'

'No, that's where you're wrong. I wouldn't love it. I don't want it,' he shouted. 'If you continue with this pregnancy, you're on your own. And don't think you can come to me for money. I won't give you a penny of my hard-earned cash!' He slammed the car door and drove away, leaving me on the pavement outside my house, shaking and sobbing.

I was on my own again, hurt and confused. Perhaps things would always go wrong in my life. Perhaps I deserved this pain and confusion.

I continued to harbour a secret hope that Larry would come round once he'd thought it through. I was still working in the pub and I knew he would be there for the New Year celebrations. Surely this would be when he came back to me? When the clock chimed twelve, he would come over. While everyone else was sharing New Year kisses, he would come over and kiss me and tell me everything would be OK.

What was it with me and hope? Why did I never learn? New Year came and my dreams went. The father of my baby danced with and kissed another woman and left me alone to watch. So that was that.

For the first few months of the pregnancy I hadn't told anyone about it, but just after New Year Mum asked me to come and stay in her house to look after Bobby while they went away on a trip and I found myself telling her about my predicament. Perhaps she would understand. After all, I had been conceived outside marriage. Maybe this would give us a common bond.

But why should she sympathise? What was in it for her?

'You stupid, stupid girl,' she snapped. 'You'll have to get rid of it. What will people say? What will they think?' She was almost talking to herself now, having dismissed me and my worries as she paced around the room. 'You will have to get rid of it and then stay away for a while.'

'I can't do that. It wouldn't be right,' I said softly, trying to calm things down. 'I don't believe in abortion.'

'Typical. That's just typical of you, having so-called high standards and ethics. Well, they won't do you any good now, my girl. Not believing in abortion won't make the alternative OK.' She stood in front of me with her arms folded and I felt as though I was seven again. Scared, confused and unloved. 'If you keep this bastard, you are on your own!'

I couldn't believe what I was hearing. How could she call my baby that name? I wanted to remind her of how I came about. I wanted to say to this woman that I would be different from her, I would love my child, no matter how he or she was conceived. I wanted to scream at her, all of these things.

But I didn't. I couldn't. I was at my lowest ebb and had no energy to fight her. So I would be on my own. Nothing new there, then. That's how it had always been. At least I wasn't totally alone now. I had Melissa, my beloved daughter, and I was naïve enough to think that everything would turn out right.

I still went round to the house sometimes to see Dad but Mum insisted that I check first that she didn't have any visitors because she was embarrassed for her friends to see my condition. I found out later that she had been telling people I had a cancerous tumour and that's why my belly was swollen. This was just one of the despicable lies she told.

I stopped working in the pub and stopped taking my antidepressants, just in case they harmed my unborn child, but soon I was suffering from horrible withdrawal symptoms that lasted for most of the pregnancy: I had terrifying dreams, hallucinations, panic attacks, and sometimes I ran from room to room crying hysterically. When I told my GP about this, he said it was just the stress. He knew my marriage was over and how this pregnancy had come about. I had been fine during my first pregnancy, when I was happily married and looking forward to the future, but he said my symptoms now were due to my changed circumstances. He didn't relate it to the fact that the antidepressants I had been on before I got pregnant this second time were much stronger than the ones I'd been taking before. He refused to believe there could be side effects when I stopped taking them. He was very concerned about my ability to cope, though, so he persuaded me to see the church adoption service, just in case.

I was determined to keep my baby, but I was so weak and tired of struggling that I went along for a meeting with them – not intending to let anyone take my child away, but to keep everyone off my back.

I was assigned a social worker since I was a single mum. This lady was very kind but told me straight how it was. She pointed out that I would have no money to bring up the new baby and that the maintenance I got from Edward for my daughter would not be enough for two children. She made me look at the reality of the situation and told me that my little girl and my unborn child would both suffer if I kept my baby. I couldn't take it in. My thinking was distorted because of the benzodiazepine withdrawal, and my sense of reason was non-existent. My life seemed to be a constant foggy battle. She was telling me that I had to choose between my precious baby girl and my soon-to-be-born baby. She persuaded me that the best thing I could do, if I loved my children, was to let the baby go for adoption.

One day, when I was eight months pregnant, the lady from the church adoption service called. She brought me a layette to take into hospital, a dozen terry towelling nappies and a bottle. She talked non-stop about the people who would give my as-yet-not-here baby a loving home.

But *I* could give my baby a home! I would love this unwanted-by-his-father baby. I thought this but didn't have the strength to say it out loud. I felt defeated. Defeated and desperately lonely.

Chapter Eighteen

When I went into labour, Edward moved into my little bungalow to look after Melissa while I was in hospital. The birth wasn't too bad this time, but the placenta wouldn't come away. The young nurse holding the little scrap of life that had just been taken from my body didn't know what to do with him when the midwife asked for her help, so she placed him in my arms. He was a boy, and so beautiful. I held on for fear of someone taking him away from me. The midwife rushed over after the birth was complete and admonished the poor young nurse, taking my son out of my arms again. The arms that were trying so hard to hold on.

They took him away, but the next day I managed to wander out of the ward and down to the nursery, where I peered through the windows until I found him. Taking care that no one saw me, or so I thought, I went in. He looked so small. Small and beautiful. And then I saw the name tag. It read 'Unknown' and that broke my heart. He wasn't unknown. I

knew him. I had known him for nine long months. The lack of
a name on his tag made it sound as though he didn't belong
anywhere.

I reached in and lifted him out of the crib. Suddenly the nursery door was flung open, he was wrenched away from me and
I was chaperoned back to my room. I couldn't cry. What would
tears have done? They had never helped me before, so I didn't
cry.

The next morning a nurse told me that the social worker
had come to take my baby away. She had in her hands the outfit
I had brought for him to go home in – a tiny white broderie
anglaise romper suit and little white socks. She placed these in
my hands then left and came back in with a carrycot holding
my precious son. I couldn't move, couldn't look.

'Would you like me to dress him?' she asked.

I couldn't speak. I was afraid of what might come out of my
mouth. But nothing would have, as there were no words to
describe how I was feeling. Or was I feeling? I don't know.
After a while, I nodded yes.

Then the social worker appeared. I was shaking at that
point; no tears, just falling apart inside.

'I want you to read the words on this card out loud,' she said
brusquely.

I looked at the card. The words that shouted out at me were
'I declare that I hand my child over to the care of the Church
of England Adoption Society.'

I couldn't do it. I couldn't say the words that took away all
my rights over my baby son. I just couldn't.

I had chosen this particular society because I thought they would be the best. Although God hadn't listened to me as a child, I had always remembered 'Suffer the little children to come unto me' from my Sunday school days. I thought God would listen this time and do what was best for my baby.

My head was swirling. I felt hot and faint. This can't be best.

The social worker was becoming impatient. 'Come on, time's ticking along. You have to take baby out of the carrycot and hand him over to me. It's for the best, you know that.'

For the best? Best for whom? Doesn't she know my heart is breaking? Can't she hear it?

The ward sister knew how hard this was for me because we'd had a chat after the birth. I looked up at her, pleading for help.

'She doesn't need to do that,' the sister said. 'I'll read the words for Cassie and she can touch the blanket. That will be enough.' She sounded firm, as though the decision was made.

'I suppose that will have to do,' came the reply. 'Let's just get on with it.'

I was shaking my head, silently sobbing – no tears, just silent sobs in my heart. The ward sister took my hand and placed it on the blanket that was keeping my baby warm, and she read the words from the card.

And then he was gone.

I don't remember what happened next. I just don't remember.

Some time later, I was taken into a room to register my son's birth. I was in a daze. I couldn't take it all in. The registrar asked his name.

'Jack,' I whispered. 'It's Jack.'

I didn't expect the next question; I wasn't prepared for it.

'His father's name?' he asked, in a matter-of-fact way.

He waited. I waited. What for? What did I think was going to happen?

'Do you have the permission of his father to name him on the birth certificate?' he asked. 'Do you have written permission?'

Of course I didn't. Larry hadn't accepted our baby, so no, I didn't have his permission.

'Then we will have to put Father Unknown.' He continued to write as he spoke. I felt dead inside.

After I got home from hospital, the next few days were a blur. I was dangerously depressed and my GP put me back on the tablets, which made me a little stronger. But it was as though there was a knife in my heart. I had this heavy burning pain inside that never left me. I couldn't sleep or eat. The only thing that kept me going was the need to look after my daughter.

About a week after my son's birth, I couldn't stand it any longer. I phoned the adoption service and asked to see him. They said it wasn't possible. I cried down the phone, but to no avail. I made many calls like this but nothing worked. Then I remembered being told that he would be in a foster home for a few weeks, before going to his adoptive parents.

I was distraught and only just functioning. Yes, I looked after Melissa and managed the home but I didn't look after myself. As a last resort I telephoned my mother. The pain I was feeling about my baby was so momentous that I suppose I hoped, in my grief, that even she would understand and want to help me. He was her grandson. Surely she would help?

But hope ran true to form. Of course she wouldn't help me.

'You're nothing to me and neither is the bastard you've given birth to. I never want to see you again, especially if you're going to get him back.' She was angry, heartless, uncaring. She went on. 'Stay away from me and my family.'

'My family,' she said. That said it all, confirmed what I had always known. I wasn't part of her family. Later I found out that she had told her friends that the baby was my ex-husband's and that it had died at birth. All she cared about was what 'people' might say.

The pain I was feeling was indescribable: an ache so great that I thought it would kill me. Physically I was drained. Even if I tried to forget I had just given birth, nature wouldn't let me. My breasts had filled with milk and were very sore. This was so cruel. I hadn't been able to feed my daughter for more than a couple of weeks because I had very little milk, but now, with no baby to suckle, I had an abundance of food to give. How could this happen? Didn't my body know that he wasn't there? Couldn't it hear my heart crying out for him?

The days were made bearable by my three-year-old daughter. It's hard to be down when you have a small child, full of energy and laughter, around you. But there were times when she sensed my grief and came to me for a cuddle. She would keep saying that she loved me, showering my face with kisses. On the rare occasions when I was able to cry tears, she would gently brush them away with her tiny hand and comfort me. She was my blessing and my sanity.

But I couldn't accept I would never see my beloved son again. I started ringing anyone I thought might know where he was. I pretended to be a social worker, a nurse from the hospital, a receptionist at the GP's surgery, anyone to try and find out where he was. And then. It happened. Pretending to be from social services, I rang the church adoption society and said I needed to call the foster parents of a child who went for adoption on 6 July and whose mother's name was Cassie Black (my maiden name). I held my breath as a woman said she would go and get the number from the file. She returned and not only gave me the telephone number but also the foster parents' address. I thanked her politely, hoping she couldn't hear my heart pounding in my chest. I put the phone down.

Thinking back, I realise how stupid my next actions were, how unfair they were on my little three-year-old girl. But back then, desperate to be reunited with my son, they didn't seem stupid or unfair at all.

The town where the foster mother lived was a few miles away. The day after I got the address, a few weeks after Jack was born, we boarded a bus to go there. Not knowing the area, I wasn't sure how far out of the town centre it would be so Melissa and I walked and walked for what seemed like miles. Then I saw it: the road where my baby son was living. The house I was looking for was towards the end. My heart was pounding in my chest, my hands were sweaty and my whole body shaking.

I hadn't looked beyond seeing him again. I didn't know what would happen or what my next move would be.

For a while I just stood there, on the opposite side of the road, holding Melissa's little hand. The house was large and surrounded by a beautiful garden. There was a pram just outside the front door. It was a hot day and someone had draped a canopy over the occupant. Was that him? Was he in there? Was it Jack?

Although I wanted to see him, to look in the pram, I was terrified and frozen to the spot. I didn't know what to do. If I went over to the pram and it wasn't him, what then? But if I went over to the pram and it *was* him, what then? Perhaps I was scared I might pick him up and run. I don't know. My emotions were all over the place. Terror filled my heart and before I knew what I was doing I began to walk quickly back down the road. I couldn't do it. I wouldn't be able to see him and then walk away. I had to try and think things through.

The next day I went to a baby shop and bought some blue booties. Again Melissa and I boarded the bus and took the long walk that led to where my baby was. I was calmer that day. I don't know why. The pram was outside and I took a deep breath, making sure no one was in sight. I told Melissa to stay where she was, on the other side of the road. It was a quiet road. I hadn't seen a car either time we'd visited. I walked towards the gate, hoping and praying that my baby son was there, in the pram. As I got closer, I knew he was. My heart racing, I bent over to see the bluest eyes I had ever seen. He was beautiful, a beautiful baby boy. My baby boy. My son.

I just gazed at him, full of love for this tiny human being. Then I began to feel scared, scared of what I might do, scared that someone would come out of the house and catch me. I placed the booties in the pram and ran back to my little girl. Now I was crying, crying like I wouldn't ever stop. I had to get home, we had to get home. She took my hand and we hurried back to the main road, and the bus that would take us back to the bungalow where we lived.

That evening I just sat and stared into space. I had no one to talk to about all of this. Was I doing wrong by seeing my baby? Was it against the law to see my son? How could it have been? I had given birth to him just a few weeks before. I felt so alone and wished yet again I had a caring mother, the kind I could confide in. I thought about everything I had been told about adoption: that it is best for the child. He would be given new parents, a new mother. But I was his mother. Couldn't I be the best?

It seems that there are winners in adoption but there is also a loser. A loser of the most momentous kind ever. Yes, perhaps it would be best for my son to have two parents and everything he needs. Yes, it would be wonderful for the family he would go to because they would have a new baby to love and care for. And yes, he would be happy. But then there was me. I had so much love to give him and all I got was pain. Pain, grief, heartache and guilt. What could I do with the feelings that were raging inside me? How could I cope with the huge, huge loss I had suffered?

I was told once that to lose a child to adoption is like losing a child to death. But it isn't. It's worse. Death is final. You grieve, accept and eventually move on. It is irreversible. When a baby is taken for adoption and placed with another mother, the grief is far harder to bear. I would always know that somewhere out there was my son. A little boy growing up in a new family. He would be unaware of me but not a day would go by without me thinking about him. Death had to be easier than that.

After a restless night I decided to go back to the house where he was living and sneak another look. Maybe this time pick him up for a cuddle. A very much needed cuddle.

On reaching the house, I waited until I was sure no one was around. Asking Melissa to stay where she was, I approached the pram.

But it was empty. I couldn't see him! It was as though my heart stopped. There was an awful, painful ache in the pit of my stomach. Before I had a chance to do anything, the door of the house burst open and I saw a lady standing there with a concerned look on her face.

'Would you like to come in?' she asked quietly. 'I presume you've come to see Jack?'

I couldn't speak. How did she know? Why wasn't she cross? What should I do now? I just shook my head and started to walk away.

'Don't go,' she called. 'Please come in and I'll make us some tea.' She looked kind.

'I have my little girl with me. I was only looking, I didn't …' I never finished the sentence, because I was fighting back the tears. I couldn't cry. If I cried now I would never stop.

'I'll get your little girl,' she replied and ushered me into the hall of her house.

When she returned with Melissa, two small children ran down the stairs and asked if she wanted to play in the garden. They skipped off happily together, oblivious to the drama that was unfolding. As we went into the kitchen, I saw a baby, my baby, just waking from his sleep, in a crib.

'He's due a feed,' his foster mother told me. 'I'll get some tea and then feed him.'

She brought the tea and a plate of biscuits over to where I was sitting. I was trying not to look in the crib, trying not to see the child I was aching for. She told me that she had seen me the first time, when I had stood opposite her house. Then the following day when she found the booties, she realised who I must be. She asked me about my daughter and myself, about the baby's father and about my life.

I could hardly speak. My voice was small and weak, but the pain in my heart was huge and powerful.

She took the tiny being out of the crib and started to give him his bottle. After a while she asked me if I wanted to give him the rest of his feed.

I nodded, totally overwhelmed.

She picked Jack up and came over to where I was sitting and placed him in my arms.

I wasn't ready for the feelings that came rushing through me. I wasn't ready for this huge gush of mixed-up emotion: fear, panic, pain and love. It took me by surprise. I thought my heart would burst.

And then the tears, oceans of them. Melissa saw this and came running in from the garden to try and brush them away.

'It's OK. Mummy isn't crying because she's sad but because she's happy,' the foster mum said. 'She'll be OK in a moment. Sometimes it's good to cry.' With that, my little girl returned to playing with her new friends.

'Would you like to talk about it?' enquired the woman who was caring for my son. 'Just tell me what you want for your baby and I'll see if I can help.'

I don't know how I managed to talk. I felt totally exhausted. The past few months had taken their toll on my resources and I was completely shattered. But tell her I did. No holds barred. I told her how my life had been up to this point, about having no love from my mother and how she refused to help me. I told of my failed marriage, the affair, the rejection and the tablets. But not about him, the evil, nasty man. I never told her about that. I couldn't talk about him. It was too huge and horrible. So I never told anyone about that.

When I was spent, physically and emotionally tired beyond description, I looked up to find this lovely lady crying with me.

'You should have kept him,' she said. 'I'll help you keep him if you like.'

Did she really say that? No one had ever said that.

'But they said I couldn't,' I whispered. 'They said it was best for him if I had him adopted and that they were concerned that I wouldn't cope and then I'd lose both of my children.'

'If you love your baby and have a home for him, there is nothing to stop you from keeping him. Nothing has been signed yet and so legally he is still yours.' She sounded confident about this. Determined to make this right. 'If you love him, he belongs with you.'

'Of course I love him. I've always loved him, but sometimes throughout all of this I haven't been able to think straight. I came off the tablets during my pregnancy so that he came to no harm but I suffered severe withdrawal. I'm fine again now.' I was feeling slightly stronger now that I had someone on my side. Someone who actually believed in me, which was a new experience for me.

She stood up and took Jack from me. I was able to let him go now that I somehow believed it was all going to work out well. This time all my prayers and all my hopes would pay off. This time I would have a happy ending.

She suggested that I go home and prepare to have my baby back. It was like a dream. I left and we went back to the bungalow to get ready for the rest of my life with my children – both of them. My son and daughter.

I had kept Melissa's pram and cot and all her baby things so I brought them down from the attic and I cleaned the pram until it shone. Then I sat down and tried to explain what was going to happen to my tiny little girl. I told her that when I had been away I had had a baby. I tried to tell her that because I wasn't well he had been living with the lady whose house we had visited. I then told her that we were going to bring him home the following day. She giggled and danced around the room, delighted with the idea. It all seemed so unreal.

I didn't sleep that night, and the following day I was in a daze. I gathered together a set of clothes that I had bought to put in the pram and then, full of excitement, apprehension, fear – I'm not sure, possibly all of those – we boarded a bus to where my precious son was living.

The foster mum was waiting for me. She made us some tea and gave my daughter a little cake. Her husband was coming home early to help with the baby's things and then they would give us a lift home.

I couldn't believe this was happening. I don't know how I got through the day. Yes, I was ecstatic that we were all going to be together, but it had been such an awful, emotionally charged ten months since I first found out that I was pregnant that I was physically and mentally drained.

We got back to my home and, after seeing that I had everything I needed, the foster parents left, promising to let the authorities know that my baby son was back with me. Back where he belonged.

That evening, feeling completely exhausted but happier than I had ever been, I bathed both children and put them to bed. Jack was in a cot in my bedroom, the same cot that Melissa had slept in when she was first born. I went to bed and lay there gazing at him, memorising him, until the early hours of the morning.

I don't remember much about the next couple of days, except that I took the children to the local shop because I needed some groceries. A friend of Larry's came out of the grocer's, looked in the pram and laughed.

'So this is his bastard, is it?' he quipped. 'Let's hope he doesn't turn out to look like his father.' Then he went on his way.

Was this what it was going to be like? Would people always see him as that? He was just a baby, a tiny baby. How could anyone be so cruel?

I'm not sure when the pain happened or how it started. I was putting the children to bed one evening when I felt strange, light-headed and suddenly terrified. My hands were sweating, my heart was pounding in my chest, and I was struggling to breathe. I was terrified. What was happening to me?

I ran into a neighbour's house, and she sat me down and called the doctor. This was to begin the chain of events that destroyed a huge part of my very being. After what seemed like hours my GP and a social worker arrived and I was taken back into my own home.

'We don't think you're coping, Cassie,' my doctor said slowly, as though if he spoke any faster I wouldn't understand. 'It has been a terrible time for you and we feel you have made the wrong decision in bringing the child back here.'

No, no mistake, I wanted to scream. It was not a mistake. But I didn't. I didn't speak, I couldn't speak. All my strength and energy had left me. I was totally mentally shattered. The social worker started to talk.

'You won't be able to afford to keep the children. You have no income, just a small amount of maintenance for your daughter. Nothing for the baby.' She said it as if it was an accusation, as if I didn't already know. She went on: 'I want you to think about what you have done. Your neighbour has said she will stay here tonight to make sure you are OK. I will see you in the morning and we will decide what to do next.'

With that she left, with my doctor close on her heels. He had given me something to make me sleep and, like a zombie, I went to bed.

The next day dawned and I wasn't sure what to expect. Back in 1971 there was no state help for unmarried mothers. The social worker was right. My only income was the small amount that Edward paid for Melissa. I had given up my job in the pub before my son was born and wasn't well enough to work at this time. Family help was non-existent and I had few friends.

As promised, the social worker arrived, along with my health visitor, a lovely lady who I liked very much. But I wasn't prepared for what happened next.

'You have two choices,' the social worker said. 'You can give up your son for adoption – not to the church society as they won't take him now, but to the social services. He will go back into care and then to the next couple on the list.'

I couldn't believe what I was hearing. Adoption was supposed to be the best option for the child. How was this the best?

But what came next shook the very core of me.

'Your other option is this.' She didn't even sound embarrassed. 'If you keep both children, if you deny your son a good start in life, the authorities will monitor you and find you wanting. You will not be able to look after all three of you on the little amount of income you have. This will mean that the children will not have adequate care. You're not well, physically or emotionally, and you have no family support. And you are also taking antidepressants. This will go against you.' I don't think she stopped to take a breath. 'So, if you insist on keeping the baby, you will possibly – no, certainly – lose both children.' She stopped now. She wasn't looking at me. She was looking at my health visitor.

'What do you mean? What will that mean for Cassie's daughter?' asked the health visitor, whom I had known for the whole of my little girl's life. 'What will happen to her? Will they both be adopted?'

I didn't know what they were talking about. It was as though I wasn't even there. The air was stuffy and I thought I was going to faint. I wasn't sure they were talking about me, me and my children. Both my children adopted? I was trapped in some kind of nightmare.

'Because the little girl is three years old and we like to keep the children together, I don't believe either of them would go to adoption,' said the now slightly red-faced social worker. 'She is older than most couples want. They would both stay in care until they were seventeen years of age.'

My health visitor came over and sat beside me. She tried to put her arm around me but I moved out of her reach.

'You have to make a choice: either give up your son for adoption, or we will eventually take both children. We have lots of parents eager to take baby boys. He will have a wonderful home, a wonderful mum.' She actually smiled at this point.

I wanted to shout at her that no one was taking any of my children away. No one would separate me from them again. I wanted to shout that he had a wonderful home, he had a mum. Me.

But I didn't. I couldn't move, couldn't speak. Couldn't function. After a long empty silence, a little voice from somewhere said, 'I can't lose my little girl. She's my life.' That's all I said.

After what seemed like an eternity, both women in the room accepted that I would keep my daughter, which meant that I would have to let them take my son. They talked between themselves for a while, and my health visitor became quite upset.

'Two weeks?' she asked the social worker. 'But that's cruel.'

The other woman looked annoyed. 'That's the soonest we can do it. We are having to make right the wrong that she did by taking back the child. He wasn't on our lists so we have to start from scratch and find a foster parent for him as an emergency!'

They were discussing my son's future as though I wasn't there. I don't think I have ever felt as bad as I did at that time. Throughout the abuse, which was unrelenting and horrific, throughout my life without any motherly love or guidance, I had felt the deepest despair and loneliness. But this was different; this time I was completely broken. Completely shattered. Devoid of all feeling and all emotion.

I was told that I would have to keep my son with me for two weeks until they found a suitable foster home. Then they left.

I couldn't look at him. I didn't want to see the look in his beautiful blue eyes. He didn't know what was happening. He didn't know that he was to be taken away from me again and placed somewhere else. And then my precious little girl – what would I tell her? How could I tell her that her baby brother was leaving us? She knew how much I loved him. What would I say? What would we do now?

True to their word, these so-called health professionals left him with me, while I knew that they were going to take him away again soon. It was the most awful time. I cared for him but showed no emotion. I bathed and fed him but I didn't play with him. I tried not to look at him any more than I had to. He would sit in his little chair and I brought it into whatever room I was in but I wouldn't look at him. I couldn't hold him. The pain sometimes lessened and in its place was this horrid numb feeling. Heavy and yet empty. My GP increased my medication. He said it would make me feel better but really it just enabled me to get through the days.

And then I had a brainwave. From somewhere, hope returned. I decided to contact my baby's father. I would ring Larry and ask him to come round.

What did I think would happen? That he would see our baby and fall into my arms and that we would live happily every after? Stupid, stupid fool.

I contacted a friend of his, as I had no idea where he was living at that time. I rushed around and tidied the place and made sure my baby boy looked wonderful. Surely he wouldn't be able to resist him? Everything would be fine after all.

Then I got a phone call from the friend. Larry had heard already that I'd brought our baby home but he wasn't coming over, he was never coming near us. Hope was shattered again.

I don't really remember much about the following days and nights. I know I didn't sleep. I had to answer Melissa's questions about why we couldn't keep our baby. Why he was going to another mother? It was breaking my heart. What was I doing to these two beautiful children? I knew then that I had no choice. I had to give him a chance of a good life, to enable me to give my little girl a good life. I shouldn't have had to make that choice, but I did.

When the day came, I asked my neighbour to look after Melissa and to keep her at the back of the house so that she didn't see him go. I wasn't ready. How do you get ready for parting with your precious son? My health visitor was the first to arrive, and then the social worker drove up in a large estate car, a Volvo. I have hated those cars since that day.

My son was in his pram in the back garden. A tiny elephant and a tiny brown bear were hanging from the front of the hood.

'Go and fetch him then,' the social worker said abruptly. 'We haven't much time.'

I went into the garden, feeling as though I was about to break apart. I reached into the pram for this tiny scrap of life I was about to lose. As I lifted him out, he grabbed at the elephant and it broke off the hood. I was devastated. Did he know what was happening? Did he want to stay? Was he hurting too?

With my heart breaking, I carried my son out to the waiting car. But then I stopped. It wasn't right. I couldn't do it. Why didn't someone come and help me?

But there was no one. My health visitor tried to coax me to place my baby in the carrycot in the back of that awful car. I couldn't do it. I wouldn't let go of him. There was a struggle as the social worker tried to pull Jack out of my arms, while I resisted and started to scream.

'No, you can't take him. He's mine. I won't let you. Please. Oh, please.'

This was the point when my heart broke. I tried to hold on to my baby son, the child I had given birth to only weeks before, but I failed. He was placed in the carrycot and the car pulled away.

I fell to the ground sobbing.

It was over. All I had left was a lifetime of guilt and regret. A lifetime of missing him.

A few weeks later I asked to see him one more time. He was still in foster care. Because I had been so ill and depressed, my GP asked social services to arrange a final supervised meeting at his surgery. I was so excited. I still hoped that someone would force them to change their minds. I thought that when I saw him everything would be OK.

When they put him in my arms I felt such love and such pain. Then reality came to me like a bolt out of the blue. Of course things wouldn't change. Of course 'they' wouldn't change their minds. He was to be adopted. I stood up and carried him into the garden. Was there a back entrance? For one fleeting moment I thought I could run away with him. Where to? I didn't know. Just run. I was hurrying to the bottom of the surgery garden, hoping to find a gate. Hardly breathing. But the social worker appeared and quickly took him from me.

It was over.

No more hope.

I knew then that things weren't going to change. He wasn't coming back to me, ever. I had lost him for good.

Chapter Nineteen

G rief is a terrible emotion. It eats away at you until the very soul of you is destroyed and permanently damaged. The next few months were like living in a horrible murky smog. I was taking a large dose of tablets, which numbed my emotions, but still I couldn't stop thinking about Jack. I avoided prams, avoided places where mums take babies. I concentrated on looking after Melissa, and in the evenings after she went to bed I would just sit without moving. I couldn't cry, I couldn't even think about crying.

The weeks went by and autumn was turning to winter when the social worker turned up on my doorstep again one day. In my confused state I thought at first that maybe Jack was being sent back. Maybe his new parents didn't want him any more. Unbelievable things had happened to me in my life. Why shouldn't something unbelievable happen again, only this time something unbelievably good? But good didn't happen to me.

'Your son's new parents would like something from you, Cassie,' she said, as though she were asking for a reference.

Hadn't they already had enough from me?

'They have asked for a letter to keep and give to the baby when he is grown up. Something from you, his biological mother.' She spoke as though she were doing me a great favour.

I wanted him to know about me. I wanted him to know me in person, but that couldn't happen. If a letter was all I could give him, then that's what I would do.

Over the next few weeks I tried to write a letter for Jack, but it was so hard. What do you say to someone you have lost forever? How do you tell them that your heart is breaking? I would start it and then have to walk away.

One day while I was coming home from town on the bus with Melissa I saw Larry, the father of my son. He was standing next to a car he had bought just before he walked out of our lives. I don't know what was going through my mind, but I rushed off the bus and over to where he was standing, taking my little girl with me. He looked up and, seeing it was me, ran over to where his works van was parked and sped off at top speed.

I was angrier than I had ever been. I could feel the fury rising in my tummy. What happened next, I don't know exactly. I vaguely remember picking something up from the ground and running towards the car. I know he loved that car. He'd brought it round to show me just before he ended the relationship, when I refused to have a termination. It was his dream car; he had always wanted one. So I know he loved it.

The next thing I know is that I arrived back home again feeling sick. Melissa seemed upset and confused. I was hot and sweaty and needed to take a bath, so I took a bath with my daughter. She always enjoyed this. We played in the bubbles and the world seemed a long way away. After she was tucked up in bed, I sat in my bedroom trying to think about the day. I knew something had happened but I didn't know what it was. My heart was beating hard and I felt scared. What had happened while we were out? I had a feeling I had done something but I didn't know what.

The doorbell rang. I wasn't expecting anyone and was reluctant to answer but then I heard a voice I recognised: it was the friend whom I had asked to contact Larry for me when I had Jack at home. Apparently Larry had phoned her to say that his beloved car had been damaged. The word 'coward' had been scratched across the windscreen. He was mortified. But what she said next shook me and I had to sit down. He had seen me running towards him and so had a neighbour. When he went back to his flat in the evening, his neighbour told him I had done it. She had seen me.

I couldn't have done that. Could I?

I was scared, because I knew it was a criminal act.

'He'll have to go to the police, won't he?' I asked in a timid, terrified voice. 'He'll probably enjoy that.'

'I asked him about that,' my friend told me. 'And he said he won't do it. Perhaps he feels deep down that he deserved it. If he reported what you had done, the whole sorry story would come out, and where would that leave him? No, he won't report it. He just said to tell you that he knows it was you.'

I was shocked to the core that I didn't remember what I had done. How could someone do something so awful and not remember? What was happening to me? I had done that with my little girl watching and I had absolutely no recollection of it. What sort of state must I have been in?

That's when I realised that I needed help to move on and change my life. The following day I went to see my doctor. I told him what I had done and that I had no memory of it. He said that possibly, because of the stress and trauma of losing my baby, I had 'flipped', as he put it, momentarily lost control. He changed my medication and said I would soon feel much better. He also offered to write to the local council to get me housed away from where all of this had happened.

The next day Edward and I decided to put the bungalow up for sale.

It was only then that I was able to write my letter for my son. It was a poem, three pages long. When the social worker came to collect it, I asked if the adoptive parents would keep his elephant toy and the clothes he'd been wearing on the day he left me and give them to him along with the poem when the time was right. She rang later and said they had agreed with my wishes. She also said that he was to keep the name Jack, the name I had given him. But that didn't help, not one little bit.

Melissa and I moved into a council house. They allocated us a three-bed one for some reason and I couldn't help thinking how neatly little Jack would have fitted in there with us. If I'd had a three-bedroom house at the time would that have made any difference to the social worker's attitude? Probably not.

It was hard, but gradually I began to meet people and make a social life for myself. A friend of my brother Tom's moved in next door with his wife and two daughters. Then an old college pal tracked me down and invited me to a party she was having. A neighbour said she would look after Melissa for the night, so off I went. And there I met a man called Robert, a carpenter, who was strong, good-looking, funny and seemed kind. We started dating and within a few months I had moved in with him. He seemed to get on well with Melissa and told me he loved me – and I needed to be loved so very much at that time. I was still on very strong doses of medication that left me befuddled and numb, but I thought I was making a good decision.

The first indication that all was not as it seemed came after about a year when I broached the subject of fighting through the courts to overturn the adoption of my baby boy.

Robert was shocked. 'You can't do that,' he said, sounding alarmed. 'He's not yours now. You can't do that.'

'But he *is* mine, he's my son. Now we're together, perhaps they would let me have him back?' I was getting upset, the feelings of panic rising. 'It won't make a difference to us.'

'That's where you're wrong,' he shouted. 'Of course it would. If you try and get him back, perhaps we should think about calling this off.'

I wanted to shout that it wasn't fair. Couldn't he see my grief, my pain? But I didn't say anything. Perhaps he was right. I was being selfish. I think I knew, really, that the authorities wouldn't change their minds anyway. There was nothing I could do. So I did nothing.

Soon after this, I was sick one morning and realised that I was pregnant. Robert was over the moon about the news and we decided to get married. He also said he wanted to adopt Melissa so she would be just as much his child as the new baby, so we organised that. I registered with his doctor and it was agreed that I could stop taking my tablets because I was concerned about the effects on my unborn child.

The pregnancy was awful; I was suffering acute withdrawal from the drugs and became very depressed. Being pregnant brought back all the memories of my previous pregnancy and the awful things that happened after my son was born, and I struggled to cope.

When my baby daughter Lucy was born, she was immediately rushed away to an incubator because she was blue and they thought she might have a heart problem. The next day when she was finally brought in to me, I couldn't stop crying. The midwife, who had read my notes, thought I was crying because the baby was a girl.

'You were wanting a boy to make up for the previous one, weren't you?' she asked. 'The one you lost.'

But I didn't 'lose' him! What was she talking about? And how could anything make up for him? She couldn't understand that my grief for my son and my joy for my daughter were all mixed up. I was happy and I was sad at the same time. Nothing would make up for my loss. Nothing. But no one would ever take my baby daughter Lucy away from me.

Robert had promised to love Melissa, to treat her the same as any other children we might have, but he didn't. After Lucy was born I noticed a definite cooling in his attitude towards my elder daughter. Both he and his family began to treat her differently from Lucy and her cousins. I spoke to him about my concerns but he did nothing about it, and that hurt me. I wasn't going to allow my little girl to feel different, the odd one out in the family, the one who didn't belong, just as I had grown up feeling. The echoes were too familiar, too sad.

We began to argue. Our sex life wasn't good because for some reason my childhood issues were coming to the front of my mind a great deal at this time and so I had difficulties making love, which Robert couldn't understand because I never explained it to him. Much of my life was in a daze from the tranquillisers I was on. I looked after my children and my home, but it was a constant struggle.

Lucy, our baby, had a serious hip problem that was only discovered after numerous visits to a paediatrician. She screamed and cried all the time, she wouldn't sleep and I knew she was in pain, so I kept going back to the doctors insisting they look into it, even though I sensed they thought I was neurotic. After an X-ray showed she had a condition called hip dysplasia, she had to wear a splint that kept her legs wide apart the whole time, making it very difficult to transport her around. What with the drugs, the endless visits to hospital and the rows about Melissa, life became fraught.

Robert also kept me short of money. I would have to sell things to buy clothes for the girls. We had a nice home that he had bought for us, he had savings and investments, and to other people he was a generous man, but he was mean with house-keeping and I knew that if I refused to have sex, then I wouldn't get the housekeeping at all. I felt trapped. Life was becoming intolerable. Then one night I must have missed taking the Pill and became pregnant again. This time I wasn't full of joy. This time I was exhausted and worried that our marriage wouldn't survive.

The doctor suggested I consider a termination because he said he was concerned for my health and thought that the hip problems Lucy had could be genetic. I needed proof of this. He arranged for us to see a genetics expert, who told us he could see no evidence that the unborn child should have any prob-lems. So that was that. I was going to keep it and I began to get excited about the prospect of a new baby.

Then, when I was five and a half months pregnant, I felt unwell one morning and phoned my doctor, who said she would be round later. I knew something was wrong and asked my friend to have the children. I told Robert how scared I was and asked him to stay with me, but he went to work anyway. I phoned my doctor again and she said she would come out after surgery. The pain was intense. I struggled upstairs to the bath-room and there, on my own, I lost my baby. The child they wanted me to get rid of. The child I had grown to love. The child whose lifeless body was lying on the cold bathroom floor.

I didn't look. I couldn't look.

When the doctor came, she scooped up the little body and forced me to look at it.

'It will help you to see this, Cassie. Just take a quick look.'

I didn't want to, couldn't face it, but when I did finally find the courage I could see that my baby had a huge head and what looked like a twisted spine. It was a little boy and he had spina bifida and hydrocephalus. It seems nature had taken control and let him go, rather than see him suffer. Yes, it did help, eventually. But on that day, the day I lost another son, it didn't help at all.

For some strange reason, my parents came over that evening. My neighbour and friend, Christine, had phoned them. Mum had never visited my house before and she had shown no interest in my marriage or my baby girl. So why now? What did she want? What was she going to do?

Soon after she arrived, Mum started crying and Christine had to comfort her. She didn't know about my mother. I hadn't told her how unloved I had been as a child and about the cruelty of this woman. As Christine comforted her, I saw Mum glance in my direction. Not in concern, not in love. She was happy because she was the centre of the universe and all the care and concern were for her. Even at this awful time, she was play-acting. She had an audience in the midst of a drama. Suddenly my miscarriage was all about her.

Dad tried to show his love for me but I wasn't sure I agreed with his sentiments. 'It's just a test,' he whispered. 'It's God testing you.'

'Why would God test me? Why did he let me become pregnant if he was going to take my baby away?' I cried.

'He knew how burdened you were and how hard life has been,' he went on, 'and he was testing to see if you would take the easy way out.'

'What do you mean?' I was getting upset and a little bit angry.

'God was testing to see if you would have an abortion or not. That would have been the easy way out. And you didn't,' he replied.

'So why did he let me lose the baby after I had refused the termination?' I went on, confused.

'Perhaps it was because you chose not to have the termination that God made the decision for you. He tested you, don't you see?' Dad clearly seemed to believe this.

I think he was trying to help me but it didn't work. I left it there, still confused, still upset and still angry.

After this I became very depressed and was put back on medication again. I managed to look after my children, but the marriage was going from bad to worse so I devoted all my time to being a good, loving mum. However, at around the age of nine, Melissa's behaviour changed and she started to become disruptive in school. I knew it was because she felt unwanted and unloved by Robert and his family, but I didn't know what to do about it.

We attended family therapy and the psychiatrist straight away identified a problem between Robert and Melissa. We all went a few times, then Robert said he didn't need to come with us any more. He said the unit doctor had told him that I was suffering from postnatal depression and grief from losing my two sons. He had persuaded the staff that he was fine, and that I was the one with the problems. They obviously agreed with him and somehow the tension between him and Melissa had been forgotten. Perhaps they were right; perhaps I did need help. But we had come there as a family, to be treated in a family unit, and somehow, for reasons I couldn't understand, I found I was being admitted to hospital as a voluntary in-patient.

It wasn't so bad to begin with; in fact, it was good to have a rest. I had the children with me all day and got some much-needed sleep at night. But then things changed. I was kept in bed in a room on my own and I only saw the girls for ten minutes each evening. I wasn't allowed visitors or phone-calls, only letters. It was horrible. I didn't understand why they were doing it. Why was I a prisoner?

In desperation, I told them that my mother had been poorly so they let me ring her. I told her what had happened and begged her to help me. I told her how scared I was and how I felt that my past had affected my judgement and that I desperately needed her help. How stupid was that? Why was I still hoping for help from her after all these years?

Her voice made it obvious that she was pleased to be able to refuse me her help yet again. 'You've made your bed,' she said. 'Now lie in it.' She really did hate me.

My medication had been increased and I was taking tablets to make me sleep, tablets to wake me up, tablets and tablets and tablets! Robert refused to help me get out because he said it was 'for the best'.

I was at my wits' end. All the staff saw was a terrified, anxious woman who wouldn't go along with their orders willingly. I didn't want to take the tablets. I didn't want to stay in bed. I *wanted* to see my children for longer than ten minutes a day. I *wanted* to go home.

I was in this unit under these conditions for six awful months. Then during one of Robert's visits he told me that he was going to apply for custody of the girls, sell our house and move away. He could do that because he had legally adopted Melissa.

'It's for the best,' he said. 'I've been looking at a school where your daughter can board, a convent school, not too far away, and then she'll only be home in the holidays.'

That said it all. *My* daughter. I was shocked.

'You can't do that. I won't let you.' I tried to sound strong, but he seemed to take it for granted that he could get his own way. What could I do, shut away in there?

I wrote a letter to my solicitor. A nurse refused to post it for me so I had to get another patient to sneak it into town to a post box. He came to see me as soon as he could, and immediately raised an injunction against the sale of the house. He also took steps to make the girls wards of court as a temporary arrangement to prevent them from being taken away. I felt better about this. And he told me that, contrary to what I had been made to understand, the psychiatric unit could not keep me against my will. I could go home any time I wanted to.

The following day I discharged myself. It was July 1977, Jubilee year. I had missed all the celebrations and street parties but I was home, where I belonged. Back with my beloved children.

My marriage to Robert staggered on for a little while longer, but it was doomed. There were just too many problems, and there were faults on both sides. My dependence on the drugs that were being prescribed for me by the medical profession, the drugs that made me befuddled and confused, was definitely a factor. Eventually we separated and I faced life as a single mother yet again.

Chapter Twenty

Once again I had to rebuild my life, but I seemed to be tired the whole time and felt generally unwell. Then one day I collapsed in the local shopping centre and my GP was called out to see me.

After examining me, he said that my body was saying enough was enough: I was to stop the tranquillisers and any other drugs I was taking. This was the same doctor who had said I would always need tranquillisers, that I couldn't function without them. This was the doctor who had told me the new pills were completely safe and non-addictive and that's why I'd been happy to take them. I didn't get the awful lows that I had experienced before, and I didn't break down and sob the whole time. Now he was telling me just to stop taking them. How was I supposed to do that?

But he was the doctor and he told me I had to, so I did. What happened next was horrific. The first two days weren't too bad but on the third day I awoke in a cold sweat. Panic overcame me and I shook so violently that I couldn't stand. All that day I felt as though nothing was real, as though I was standing outside myself looking in. That night I had dreadful nightmares. I awoke to the walls closing in on me and I was terrified – of what, I didn't know. Over the next two days I lapsed in and out of terror, panic, sickness and violent shaking fits. At one stage I went out into the garden naked and tried to dig a hole in the soil with my bare hands so that I could hide in it. Then I cut my head on a wall during a panic attack. I couldn't see clearly. One minute I couldn't move and the next I was running from room to room like a creature possessed. I spent the sixth night huddled in my cloakroom, desperately trying to crawl under the S-bend of the toilet and wanting to die.

Finally a close friend took me back to my GP. I looked dreadful. I'd lost a lot of weight and had barely slept during the week. I told the doctor what had happened and asked him for help, but he told me categorically that there were no withdrawal effects with benzodiazepine drugs. He didn't believe that what I was suffering was caused by the tranquillisers. He thought it was all in my mind but said that if I couldn't pull myself together then I had better keep taking the tablets.

I went home feeling broken. If what the GP said was true, I must be going insane. I decided that enough was enough. I could take no more. My head was exploding with the cruelty, the abuse, the failures. I couldn't continue like this. Perhaps I should finish it.

What happened next is a blur. My girls were at a friend's house, so I knew they would be out of the way. I took the tablets that this doctor had given me and started to swallow the amount he had prescribed. I'm not sure what I was going to do next – I don't think I was going to take an overdose – but before I had taken very many pills a friend of mine arrived and, seeing my distress, she called an ambulance. It could have been a cry for help – who knows? The ambulance men were very understanding and made sure I was OK then left. If it hadn't been for them, and my friend, I might not have survived. But I was alive – and back on the pills.

Over the next weeks and months I didn't seem able to think straight because of the medication but decided that if I had to stay on it for life, then that's the way it had to be. For years it had been part of my daily routine to check that I had enough pills with me before I left the house. Most women check their bags to make sure they have their purse and keys; I checked for my tablets. When I needed more, I just rang the surgery, collected a prescription the next day and took it to the chemist. No questions asked, no hesitation. I would just have to carry on this way because I couldn't face the alternative.

After things settled down again, I decided to look for a job and soon found one, working as a receptionist in an accountancy firm. I enjoyed the work and knew I was good at it. There was a nice bunch of people there and I was treated well.

Then, after the firm's Christmas dance, one of the junior partners, a man called John, gave me a lift home and kissed me on the doorstep. He was very attractive and I knew lots of the girls at the office fancied him, so I was flattered. I'd got the impression previously that he was married but he told me that he and his wife were separated and filing for divorce, so that was OK. We had a whirlwind romance from the Christmas of 1981 and got married in July 1982. My mother actually came to this wedding, so impressed was she by John's exalted career and secure financial status. At last her failure of a daughter had married someone with money and position, and she was delighted.

I should have recognised that the drugs I was taking had affected my powers of reason and judgement. I knew that I wasn't really functioning properly, but I was so desperate to be loved and wanted that I was vulnerable to making the wrong decisions, the wrong choices.

It wasn't long before my fairytale marriage began to lose its lustre. First of all I had a call from the manager of the hotel where we'd had our wedding reception to say that the bill hadn't been paid. John tried to lie his way out of this before confessing to me that he had 'forgotten'. Then I found out that he hadn't been paying the insurance premiums and when one of my cats fell through the roof of our neighbours' conservatory and they charged us for the damage, it turned out that we weren't covered. When I confronted John about this, he lost his temper and started hitting out at objects round the house. What else didn't I know about?

A few weeks later I was out with some girlfriends on a hen night when a man came over and called me a marriage wrecker. I had no idea what he was talking about. He explained that he was John's ex-brother-in-law and dropped the bombshell that his sister's marriage to John had only broken up after she

I did tell, I did

discovered that he was engaged to me! I had no idea that John was still living with his wife when he asked me to marry him, but lots of things fell into place at that moment and I realised it was true.

What this man said made sense of a few things that had worried me or confused me during my engagement. But I never for one minute thought John was still married whilst we were planning our wedding. I knew he could lie – he had been doing that throughout our very short marriage – but this was different, this was unforgivable. By lying to his wife, he had implicated me. How dare he!

'I don't know what you're talking about,' John said when I confronted him. 'You've got the wrong end of the stick. Whoever told you needs to get their facts straight.'

'It was your brother-in-law, your wife's brother. He should know. He said she was devastated and had a breakdown when she found out about us.' I could feel the panic rising in my stomach. 'How could you do this, to her and to me?'

I wasn't ready for what happened next. I didn't see it coming. But I felt it.

I reeled back as the force of his hand knocked me off my feet. Did he just do that? How could he? How could he hit me? I hadn't done anything wrong.

The following day he said he was sorry. I was still in shock. This couldn't go wrong. I couldn't have another marriage break-up – my third. I had to make it work. I had to believe him. I tried to tell myself that it was a one-off, that it wouldn't happen again.

But it always does. This was just the beginning of a different kind of horror.

As the days went on I found John out in many lies and he always managed to talk me round into believing he would change – but he didn't.

Then one evening as we were dressing for a party, he asked me to strip off in front of him and face the mirror. I don't know why this made me feel uneasy – perhaps it brought back horrible memories – but I refused. He became very animated and insisted I had to strip off in front of him. I was becoming scared, because he had hit me before, but I couldn't do it. I froze to the spot. He stormed across the room and threw me on the bed.

'You'll do as you're told,' he growled.

He tore off my clothes and proceeded to have sex with me. Rough, cruel sex. He kept hitting me while he groped my body. I was so scared that I let him do it, and when it was over he got up and left the room.

I couldn't cry. This was too big for tears. I felt numb and drained. I felt like a little girl again. A frightened, abused little girl.

This was the start of a pattern of brutal sex, sexual assault and violence. It was exactly like revisiting my past. I tried to blank out what was happening, and spend my days pretending that things would be OK. I was expert at that. I knew what to do. Just wait, and it would be over soon.

I very quickly learned to read the signs. For example, I knew it was about to happen if he came home from work and locked both the front door and the back. If I didn't object, I told myself, if I went along with his wishes, he wouldn't be too violent, and the quicker I gave in, the sooner it would be over.

Then one afternoon I was putting things away in the wardrobe when I saw what I thought was a book, hidden under a jumper. I suppose I shouldn't have looked, but I did. When I reached up the whole pile came tumbling down and I couldn't believe what I was looking at on the floor in front of me. Porn films! Not just soft porn but films with disgusting covers that made me feel sick. I quickly put them back. I didn't want to look at them, didn't want to touch them. How could he have such things in the house where my girls lived? Melissa was fourteen now and Lucy was just nine, and they could have been deeply disturbed by these images. How dare he bring them into my home? Did he watch these when he was downstairs after I had gone to bed, then come up and have sex with me? I felt ill.

Flashbacks filled my mind. Flashbacks of the abuse and cruelty I suffered as a little girl – a little girl who had no choice but to suffer the things that were happening to her.

But I wasn't a little girl now and I didn't have to endure this. I didn't want them in my home; I didn't want him in my home!

That evening, when I confronted John, he said he was just storing the videos for a friend of his.

'How dare you bring them here, with my little girls in the house?' I cried. I knew I had every right to be angry. But again I wasn't ready. I didn't see it coming. Before I could blink, he was grabbing at my hair.

'You're hurting me, stop it!' I cried, trying not to raise my voice in case it woke the girls.

'I haven't started yet,' he shouted, grabbing me even harder. 'How dare you look at my private things?' He let go of my hair and slapped me hard across the face.

I'd had enough; I pushed him out of the way and ran into the hall, aiming to get out the front door, but he shoved me against the banisters and put his hand around my neck, compressing it. I was terrified because he seemed like a man possessed. Then I looked up and saw my girls, my precious children, cowering at the top of the stairs.

That was the turning point; this had to stop. With all my strength, I kicked out at him and managed to break away. I yelled up at the girls that they should go into their bedroom and close the door, then I sprinted out the front door and ran as fast as I could to the nearest phone-box, where I rang John's mother. We had a tense relationship, because she was a doting mum who thought her son could do no wrong, but I rang her anyway because I didn't know who else to call. I told her what had happened and asked her to ring John immediately and bring him to his senses.

When I got back to the house there was no sign of John but the girls were cuddled up together in the bedroom and it was evident they had been crying. I comforted them as best I could until I heard John coming back with his mother. Surely she would have to stick up for me after what he had done? Surely she would tell him to go and I would be safe.

But no.

The surprise words from her were that *I* had to go. She didn't believe me; she didn't want to believe me. He was her son.

'I want him to leave,' I said firmly. 'I want him to leave right now and never come back. Our marriage is over.'

'He isn't going anywhere,' his mother said, sounding very smug. 'This is his house, he pays the mortgage, so he is staying. You'll have to leave.'

'I can't. I have the girls, I have nowhere to go.' Fear gripped me for a moment.

'That's not our problem,' his mother continued cruelly. 'He deserves someone much better than you, and you know it.'

Surely someone too good for me wouldn't have lied throughout our marriage? Someone too good for me wouldn't have slapped and punched me. Someone too good for me wouldn't have tried to strangle me. At first I said nothing, then my neck started to sting. I put up my hand to touch the place where he had compressed my throat and that gave me the strength.

'Yes, I'll go,' I told her. 'I'll go straight to the police station and tell them of the punches and slaps I have taken over the last six months. I'll show them my throat!' I took my hand away to show her the marks, and my husband's mother gasped in shock and disbelief.

They both left.

The following day, upset and shattered, I started the proceedings to file for yet another divorce. I thought I had got it right this time but the man I married wasn't what he pretended to be. The charm was all on the surface. Perhaps my judgement had been impaired all along. I kept making the same mistakes and getting hurt over and over again, so perhaps it was me. This couldn't go on. Things had to change.

Ever hopeful that one day my mother would be supportive of me and her granddaughers, I rang to tell her the news. When she heard what had happened she slammed the phone down on me, but not before saying that everything must be my fault and that John was blameless. What did I expect? Why did I even bother? The only person who could make changes in my life was me.

A few days after John moved out, I watched a TV programme that was to change my life. It was *That's Life*, presented by Esther Rantzen, and it was about dependency on GP-prescribed drugs and the problems people have stopping them. For me it was a huge wake-up call. I had been on medication for twenty-four years by that stage, a lot of the time in a fog of confusion, as though my head was filled with cotton wool. The pills had originally been prescribed to deal with headaches but they had messed with my mind, making me unable to function properly and affecting my reason and judgement. Perhaps my relationships were doomed to failure because of my inadequacies and my drug-filled life, or perhaps the men I had chosen just didn't understand me. I don't know, but I vowed that this last marriage would be my last mistake. Life had to change and I had to change it. I had to come off everything – all the poison that was destroying my life – and live drug-free. Then, if I made mistakes, it would all be down to me.

The producers of *That's Life* wanted people to take part in a survey and offered to send leaflets to help sufferers break the habit. I sent for the pack that was on offer and was hugely encouraged by it. Armed with their literature, a great deal of determination and little else, I went to my doctor's surgery. It was the same practice but I saw a different partner to the one I had seen before. I told him what the other GP had told me, about having to remain on medication for life. I went on to say that although I would appreciate his help and support, with or without it I was going to beat the habit and come off everything. This was my last chance. Although he was a bit sceptical, he agreed to see me regularly during what he said would be a very difficult time. So he knew of the dangers! Why hadn't someone told me?

I was taking huge doses of anti-anxiety medication and antidepressants, and I knew I would have to cut down slowly or I would suffer unbearable withdrawal. With the help of the *That's Life* leaflets, I worked out a gradual reduction programme and, following their advice, I sat the girls down and told them what I was going to do. They were so supportive that I was very proud of them. They weren't scared, but were very matter of fact as we discussed the practicalities and how they could help. I hoped it wouldn't affect them adversely to see me in my worst state, but all I could do was protect them as much as I was capable of.

At first, as the drugs were reduced I began to feel very weak and had fits of shaking and cramps in my legs and arms. One evening, after about a week of withdrawal, I suddenly felt terrified and ran from room to room, not sure what I was running from. My skin was clammy and sticky and I felt so ill that I rang a friend.

'I think I'm going to die!' I cried. 'I can't do this. I must take something.'

That was the last thing I wanted to do but the fear and the physical symptoms were so awful that I wanted to stop trying to stop.

'You can do this, Cassie,' my friend said firmly. 'You know you can, I know you can. We'll work through it.' Encouraged by her strength and feeling safer because she was there, I saw it through. She held onto me while I shook violently and then slumped, exhausted, into her arms.

This was the first of many such panic attacks and bouts of terrible, inexplicable fear. A few days later, having reduced my dose very slightly by breaking the pills into pieces, I suddenly felt violently giddy and began to hallucinate, seeing black slimy things crawling out of the walls of my home. It was horrific. I was so scared that my whole body began to shake and jerk in rapid movements. I thought I was going mad. I thought I was going to die.

The physical problems that were part of the withdrawal included constipation and indigestion. I took herbal remedies for both, but to no avail. I couldn't sleep because of the shaking and nausea I was suffering. As I reduced the dose of one particular drug, I suffered complete muscular seizures. My body went absolutely rigid and my jaw felt as though it were locking. I was terrified. Along with this, sticky yellow stuff was being secreted in my underwear. It was the most horrible feeling, as though my body wasn't my own. I would wash for what seemed like hours and still I never felt clean. Of course, this brought back all the fear and terror that I had felt as a little girl, when I had been sexually abused by Uncle Bill. I had vivid flashbacks to the times when I used to rush to the safety of the bathroom after his attacks, lock the door and scrub between my legs until it hurt. I might be a grown woman now but it felt the same, and all the memories and feelings of childhood came flooding back. Association is a very powerful force.

In between these times, I had severe panic attacks and would run round the house sobbing and screaming until I was exhausted and would fall in a heap onto the floor. Sometimes at night I would manage to get off to sleep but then I would wake, terrified, not knowing why. The walls of the bedroom would feel as though they were closing in on me and I was suffocating. I couldn't breathe properly. I just wanted it to end.

I couldn't eat properly and lost a great deal of weight. Melissa and Lucy would bring me raspberries or chocolate to try and tempt me to eat. Melissa took over the housekeeping and shopping while Lucy spent time with me, encouraging me to keep on with the programme I had set myself. Little notes would appear – 'You can do it, Mum' or 'We love you, Mum' – to encourage me to keep going. They really were stars during this awful time.

On Christmas Day, after I had been awake all night, I suddenly had the panic attack of all panic attacks. The hallucinations were horrible: I thought I saw bodies all over the floor, oozing blood. Flashbacks of the abuse, memories that I couldn't escape, were rushing through my mind. I was banging my head against the wall of the bedroom just trying to knock all the thoughts that were haunting me out of my head. I ran out of the house and began to make my way to my friend's house, two streets away. The horrors I was feeling stripped me of any common sense or sense of reality. Several people gave me strange looks as they passed but I didn't care. Then a neighbour saw me and stopped me.

'Are you OK, Cassie?' she asked with concern. 'Are you sure you should be out like this?' she continued, looking down at my clothes.

This stopped me in my tracks. I looked down and realised that I still had my slippers and dressing gown on. I hadn't washed or combed my hair. Added to the terror I was feeling at that time, I must have looked demented.

She put her arm around my shoulder to guide me back home and I crumpled to the floor sobbing.

These withdrawal symptoms continued to one degree or another for eighteen months as I reduced the tablets little by little. I alternated between not being able to sleep at all or having horrific night terrors, and the panic attacks during the day rendered me helpless and distraught. I thought it would never end. I became afraid to go to bed because of the nightmares and sometimes sat in my chair all night. I wouldn't answer the phone some days and definitely wouldn't answer the door.

As I came down further from the original dose, I realised that my self-confidence was non-existent. At least whilst I was

I did tell, I did

taking the drugs, I was able to go out and do all the things required of me. At least with the medication I could function. Most people didn't even know I had a problem. I don't think I knew I had a problem, until I tried to stop taking the tablets.

But then some of the positives began to kick in. As the amount of medication I was taking reduced, I was surprised at how different I began to feel. I could taste food again, smell perfume and flowers, and feel emotions that had been locked away.

One of the most poignant times was when I was playing with my dog one day and I laughed, laughed out loud. My daughters stopped what they were doing and stared at me. I didn't know what I had done. I just knew that something had either alarmed them or scared them.

'What's wrong?' I asked. 'Why are you looking at me like that?'

They continued to stare, not sure what to say to me.

'You laughed, Mum,' said Lucy. 'You laughed.' She sounded unsure how I was going to react. They both stood still. And then I cried and they flew over to me and hugged me.

'It's all right, Mum, it's good that you laughed, isn't it?' Melissa asked.

I assured her that it was indeed good and that I was crying with happiness, but the truth was, I was crying because of the impact that my laughter had had on my precious children. I wondered how long it had been since they had heard it.

Then one day I shouted at them. They were mortified. I hadn't shouted for years. I either didn't have the strength or just didn't become so cross that I had to shout. I hadn't become angry or stressed while taking the drugs; I didn't feel very much at all, so when I shouted at them they were shocked. So there were downsides as far as the children were concerned, but they were safe in the assurance that this was good, this was what normal mothers do.

During the last six months of breaking my dependency I needed something to focus on and decided to look for a part-time job doing something interesting but not too taxing. I was in the throes of cutting down the tablets into the smallest pieces possible and I had terrific mood swings but my concentration was improving. I was incredibly thin but had started to take a pride in my appearance once again. I laughed more and enjoyed things much more than I could ever remember doing.

I was offered a job working for two young men who ran a marketing and design company and I decided to tell my new employers my story to enable them to understand my ever-changing moods. They were incredibly supportive and suggested that I should wear a colour-coded badge: yellow on a good day, blue on a not-so-good day and red on a bad day. They wouldn't even speak to me when I wore the red badge unless I spoke first. It worked. I began to see a funny side and get my sense of humour back. I had used humour as a defence sometimes, but now I could actually laugh at myself. Both of these lovely young men supported me in my endeavour to end the dependency by showing complete faith in my ability to do this and to do my job.

I did tell, I did

The hardest part of ending the control these pills had on me was to let go of the last tiny piece of the last pill. This took months and months. I think I was afraid of the fear itself, more than afraid of what might happen. Logically I knew that the tiny piece of tablet that I couldn't let go of couldn't make very much, if any, difference. But it was like a crutch – a crutch that I was afraid to give up. I continued to take this minute piece of medication every morning. I just couldn't let go, couldn't give it up until some eighteen months after beginning to cut down. I finally gave up completely in November 1984, a year before my fortieth birthday.

It had been eighteen long months since I made the decision to go clean and it was extraordinarily difficult, but when I came out the other side I soon began to realise just how much the struggle had been worth it. At last I was myself again.

Chapter Twenty-one

As I got used to my new, drug-free life, the last thing on my mind was romance. I was done with that, permanently. I had been there several times and won all the T-shirts. Now I had a mortgage to pay, two daughters to feed and clothe, and several pets to look after, because we had somehow collected a little dog, three cats and numerous rabbits and guinea pigs. I needed to earn enough money to do all this, so that was my priority. I was promoted to a different job within the marketing and design company, and I now worked closely with the two partners who were the creators and designers. I loved the creative atmosphere and the fact that people would ask my opinion on ideas and themes for campaigns and adverts. At first I had been doing the books, then I moved into despatching goods and soon I was running the whole office. It was a very happy, productive little team.

One of the directors was a very charismatic man called Peter. I was fascinated by him right from the start as I really admired his creative brain and the work he did. One day we needed a quiet room for recording a campaign for a new product and he suggested using a room in his house, so I went back with him to assess it. It was then, on our own and out of the office setting, that I had to admit to myself that I was very attracted to him. But surely it would never be reciprocated? Surely he wouldn't look at me?

I asked the girls in the office about him and they all said that he was a very nice guy but a confirmed bachelor. He had girlfriends but he was quite clear that he would never settle down with any of them, because he liked living on his own with his Irish red setter. I wasn't looking for any serious commitments either, so that seemed ideal.

Gradually, as we worked together, he began asking about my life. I told him about my battle to come off tranquillisers and, when I finished, he leaned over and kissed me very gently. Could something good be about to happen in my life? Still I didn't dare hope. Was there no hidden agenda this time? Was God listening?

We went to a design fair together and at the end of the day we stopped for dinner on the way home – and again he kissed me. It was gentle and undemanding and I was ecstatic. I couldn't stop smiling for ages after he dropped me off at my front door. Life seemed so much brighter than it had been for years – decades, even. I had a job I loved, two wonderful daughters and now *this*. A new chance.

One afternoon when we had closed the office early, Peter asked if I would like to go for a drink. Of course I said I would love to and we drove to his house. He had the first CD player I had ever seen or heard – they were still a new technology – and as he placed the earphones on my head I felt tingly, almost drunk. Sometimes, his closeness was almost too much. The music sounded incredible and I was blown away. Up till then we had shared a few kisses but we had never made love. Again I hadn't even thought about this; perhaps I didn't read the signs or perhaps I didn't understand my own feelings. For me, sex had always been at the bidding of a man, and it was sometimes bearable, sometimes brutal, just something that I put up with for one reason or another.

Since I was a child.

Since forever.

So why would I have read the signs? This was different – not dirty, not nasty, but different.

So I didn't see it coming. It was a total surprise that I could make love with a man without the fear and dread that had always accompanied this act. But make love we did. It was a new experience for me, and afterwards I cried. Peter was mortified.

'I'm so sorry,' he said, looking at me with such warmth. 'I thought it was OK, I thought it was the right time.' He looked sad.

I didn't know what to say; I didn't know what I felt. All I knew was that something had happened to me and it felt right.

'It's OK,' I said softly, afraid that if I spoke any louder he would disappear. 'Honestly, it's OK, I'm OK.'

Without either of us speaking, we cuddled up and fell asleep. It felt safe. Later, he took me home and we didn't mention what had happened. I was confused and worried. What had happened back there? What was that feeling? I was afraid to be happy, afraid that if I accepted that I was falling in love, it would all be stolen from me. It seemed God was listening to me now, but it was so new that I was confused and a bit scared, if truth be told.

The next time we saw each other, we drank a bit of champagne and I told him of my fears and confusion. He replied with a kiss so gentle and warm that all of my previous feelings disappeared. It felt so good, so right. It felt as if there were only two people in the whole world. Him and me.

I don't know if it was the champagne but when we went to bed I lay by his side and began to cry, tiny little tears, and I told him everything. I told him of my childhood, the abuse and my being afraid to love, even that I didn't know what love was. He was the first person I had told about Bill, the only person – apart from Mum, that is – and he was horrified and sympathetic and angry all at once. He told me that none of it had been my fault; I was only a child. My fear had always been that I would be blamed, or not believed, but Peter reassured me that this was nonsense. It felt easy telling him, it seemed right. He held me until I went to sleep. I felt safe.

The following day I was sure things would be different with us. I don't know what I expected but what I didn't expect was that nothing had changed. Peter was the same, I was the same, but something was different. When he caressed my body, he was so loving and gentle that I relaxed and began to respond. He made me feel special, and this special was good. His touch was magical, like it was the most natural thing in the world, and we made the most beautiful love that could be imagined. Yes, I cried, but these tears were tears of joy.

Over the next few months this wonderful, love-bringing man taught me self-respect and self-worth. Peter loved and believed in me. Yes, the sexual side was wonderful and I began to realise that I could enjoy sex, but the whole package – being loved and the way this made me feel – changed me completely. I thought I had loved before but I knew now that I hadn't. This love was different; it was complete and good. In this love, I had grown – grown as a woman and as a person. Peter gave me confidence, confidence to be me, to do what I wanted and to be OK with the consequences. He taught me how love and sex could be wonderful. Not dirty, not nasty, not evil. He made me realise that I was capable of enjoying life and that it was OK to do so. But most of all he helped me to find me. His love was the beginning of my actually liking the person I was becoming and learning that it was OK to feel that way.

We travelled round the country together, going to design fairs, staying in hotels, and at Christmas he took me to London where we drove along looking at the Christmas lights. It was drizzling and the rain looked like tears. The lights looked smudged yet beautiful and their beauty stunned me. It was like a fairyland to my eyes. I gasped and sighed at what I was seeing.

'You're like a little girl,' Peter said kindly. 'A little girl anticipating Christmas.'

I suppose I was in a way – although as a little girl Christmas had never been worth the anticipation. But yes, I had waited for it, each year, with more hope and prayers than I should have invested. But I wasn't a little girl now; I was a grown woman, a woman in love with a man who I knew ultimately wouldn't be mine. No matter how much he loved me, he would never change his views and ask me to marry him, or even move in with him. He was a free spirit, too independent to ever be tied down. What we had was wonderful but it wasn't going anywhere. As I watched the lights fading, there was little difference between the tears of rain on the window and the salty tears running down my cheeks.

At our hotel that night, I had an idea for a story about a little character and a mirror. Peter thought the idea was really good and encouraged me to write more. This was the beginning of another dream that I had – to write for children. A few years later, with the confidence he had begun to give me and the belief in my character, a dream was realised. I wrote this story and self-published my book to great acclaim.

Early in the New Year, the design company we worked for was disbanded. Peter and I continued to work together for a while on our own projects but gradually I was coming to realise that I wanted more from a relationship than he could give. It was one of the hardest decisions I had ever made in my life but I knew I had to end things between us before I got hurt.

He was distraught when I told him. 'Don't do this,' he begged. 'We can still see each other.'

Through my tears I told him I had to. 'I want more than you can give me. I always have.' I was as honest as I had always been with him. 'You never made me any promises about commitment. You never lied about that, but I want more.'

We held on to each other for a long time, and through his tears he whispered, 'But I never got to kiss the back of your knees. I have kissed every other beautiful part of you.'

I almost changed my mind. I wanted to change my mind but I didn't. I wanted to thank him for all that he had given me. To tell him how he had changed my life, how he had changed me. I wanted so much to let him know that life was now a good place for me and it was mostly thanks to him. I wanted so much to say thank you for helping me to realise the beauty and wonder of love, both sexually and emotionally. I wanted to say that I still loved him, that I'd always love him and thank him for loving me. I wanted to say so much.

But I couldn't.

I couldn't speak through my tears.

As he left the house, I wondered if I was doing the right thing. Should I have just held on to what I had and been satisfied? Should I run after him and say everything would be all right?

But I didn't. It wasn't right. If I had stayed there, I would never have moved on to the next happy time, the next love and to the rest of my life.

Over the next few months I became a teenager again. I started going out to nightclubs and rediscovered my love of dancing. My daughters often told me off for the sexy outfits I wore – 'You can't go out in that, Mum!' they'd exclaim, to my great amusement. I had lots of dates with men, going out for dinner and even to watch the local football team playing, but none of them were serious.

Then one night, when I was out clubbing with a girlfriend, a man called Daniel came over and asked me to dance. He was dark-haired with the deepest brown eyes I'd ever seen and once I was in his arms I felt giddy and could almost hear my heart beating. I wasn't sure what was happening – I didn't want anything to happen so soon after parting from Peter. But once we got talking, we couldn't stop. We sat up chatting till four in the morning the first night we met, because there was just so much to say.

Over the next few weeks we had an old-fashioned courtship. He brought me handmade chocolates, flowers and gifts, and I could tell he was a true romantic. No pressure, no hurry, just a gentle getting to know each other.

About two months after meeting Daniel, I heard that my dad had been quite ill and, after many attempts, found the courage to ring home to ask after him. Mum hadn't been speaking to me since the end of my marriage to John. She couldn't forgive me for letting such a wealthy, prestigious man slip through my fingers, even though I told her about what he'd done to me. I used to ring to speak to Dad when I was sure she would be out but a couple of times she intercepted the calls and responded with scathing sarcasm, making me nervous about calling again. But now Dad was ill and Mum was happy to let the prodigal daughter return to help her play the role of worried wife. I visited Dad in hospital and was distraught when he told me that he was dying.

'You're not going to die, Dad. You can beat this. You've been through worse than this.' I tried not to cry, not to let him see how scared I was.

'No, my love, this time it's beaten me.' He seemed calm now, almost relieved. 'Bye, bye,' he murmured, before nodding off to sleep. These were his last words to me, as he died later that night. My beloved dad was gone. I had loved him with all my heart, even though I knew he was weak, too weak to stand up to Mum, too weak to protect me. He was a kind, gentle soul and I mourned for him.

I stayed with my mother for a few days, making arrangements for the funeral. Although in public she played the grieving widow, crying whenever someone came to offer their condolences, in private she talked and talked about the love of her life: Bill. The man who had hurt me so badly. No thought for my dad, no thought for me, just her grief for the man with whom she had had a decades-long affair. She would ask me to hold her while she cried for him and I found this very hard. She had never held me, as a child or as a young woman, but now she wanted me to hold her while she cried for my abuser.

We started clearing out Dad's things and Mum moaned about him hoarding souvenirs that we had given him as children. He wasn't long dead, but still she was berating him. She didn't behave badly to me during this time, but only because she needed me to play a supporting role in her current drama. None of her other children came to stay, so for once she needed me.

As the year progressed, so did my romance with Daniel. One evening, after we'd been playing music by candlelight and sharing a bottle of wine, we made love. This time I was ready. This time I wanted it. He was kind, thoughtful and gentle. It wasn't scary, or nasty, or bad. This time was good. Love was back, different and right. He didn't know about my past. I hadn't told him. I hadn't told my family either – except Mum. I'd told her, a long time ago when I was a child.

But now life was good. Because Daniel didn't know about the abuse and my childhood, I suppose he wasn't surprised when things were good. But I was. I knew it would happen one day, but in the back of my mind I had often wondered if it would be OK. So we made love and it was more than OK. I knew then that I loved him for all the right reasons. I knew we were going to be happy.

One evening we were going out for a meal and, in my rush to get ready, I had forgotten to put my dress rings back on my fingers. At the end of the meal I was fiddling with my bare, ringless fingers.

'Perhaps you should put this one on,' Daniel said, sliding a tiny box across the table. 'See if this one fits.'

I was taken by surprise because we hadn't discussed getting serious. I opened the box with shaky hands. Inside was a tiny solitaire, a diamond on white gold. It was beautiful.

'Which finger shall I put it on?' I asked nervously.

Daniel took my hand and placed the ring on my engagement finger. I was speechless. So much for not getting serious! There were two elderly ladies on the next table and they were sighing and smiling at us. It was a lovely romantic evening. A new memory for me to treasure.

Shortly after this, we moved into a brand new house, our first proper home together, and in 1987 we got married. Unlike my other relationships, I never rowed or argued with Daniel. Instead we laughed a lot. I could never have had this relationship if I'd still been taking tranquillisers because it was totally real and present and honest. I chose Daniel with a clear head and an open heart. He knew about my mother and how she hadn't loved me as a child; he knew that I had had to give up my beloved son Jack for adoption; he knew about my tranquilliser addiction; in fact, he knew most things. The only thing I hadn't told him was about the abuse by Uncle Bill. I couldn't bring myself to take those memories out of the closet. It didn't seem necessary any more.

I still occasionally suffered from panic attacks when I was under a lot of stress, but with the help of my new husband and my beautiful daughters I would manage to ride out the storm.

Chapter Twenty-two

Lucy and I were watching television one evening, a programme about British soldiers fighting abroad, when she suddenly remarked that we didn't even know if my son Jack was alive or dead. That was a horrible thought. What if he was dead? I would never see him again.

It was then that I made up my mind to try and find him. When I told Daniel, he was very supportive and helped me to put the wheels in motion. I contacted social services and was put in touch with a social worker called Sally, who worked in the adoption section. After looking into my case, she rang me back and said that in her opinion I had been treated very badly. According to her, my son should have been placed in foster care and I should have had open access until I was well enough to have him back.

I didn't say anything, couldn't say anything.

They got it wrong, she said. She went on to say that she would find out anything she could and report back as soon as she had anything to tell me. It was 1992, the year of his twenty-first birthday.

A couple of weeks later, Sally phoned to tell me that she had contacted Jack's adoptive father. I tried to contain my excitement as I listened to what she told me. She said that this man's wife, my son's adoptive mother, had just died, so he didn't think it was a good idea to tell his son about my 'interest in his welfare' at this stage. I agreed to leave things for a year and Sally said she would write to Jack's father again at that time.

There was someone else with whom I wanted to get back in touch: Claire, my bestest childhood friend. Before my first marriage ended and Jack was adopted, Claire and I lost touch because her husband was an officer in the Navy and they got posted elsewhere. I suppose life got in the way. Up until I was forty, my head was messed up with the tablets and my life lurched from one disaster to another. But now I was OK and life was good, my thoughts returned to the happy times of my childhood. I rang everyone in the phone book with Claire's surname and at last I tracked down her aunt. She gave me Claire's phone number and I rang her. At first I thought she sounded a bit distant, but within a few minutes we were giggling about our past. She told me that she had tried to find me years before when she was having her twenty-fifth wedding celebrations and she had asked my mother for my phone number, but was told that no one knew my whereabouts. Mum had lied, in other words. But that didn't matter any more. We were talking now, so all that was history.

I met up with Claire while she was holidaying close by and I drove to the place she was staying. Bar the odd grey hair, she had hardly changed from the days when we were kids trying on lipstick together in Littlewood's. We both stood, staring in wonder, then fell into each other's arms. We laughed and cried and talked and talked. After lunch in a local pub I took her home to meet my family and they were happy to make her welcome, having often heard me talk about my extra-special childhood friend, my bestest friend.

Eventually I met Claire's parents again when I surprised them by turning up at their ruby wedding party. Her mum cried and said how much she had missed me. She had also tried to find me through my mother, to no avail. Over the next few months we talked a bit about the past and Claire's mum told me how worried she had been about me when I was a child. She knew something was very wrong in my life, and that Mum had a very cold attitude towards me, but there wasn't much she could do to help, short of making me welcome at their house whenever I was allowed to stay. Getting back in touch with them was like putting a missing part of my family back in place and I knew we would stay in touch for life now.

There was just one more bit of my family that still had to be put in place, and the call to fix that came on a Friday afternoon in July 1993. It was from Sally, the social worker.

'Do you remember that I said I would try and find out anything I could about your son?' she asked, as though I was ever going to forget such a thing. 'We said we would wait a year, and that was thirteen months ago. I sent a letter to the adoptive father last week and he showed it to his son, your son.'

I held my breath. And?

'He would like to meet you.'

I couldn't believe it. I was shaking with excitement, fear, apprehension, and a combination of twenty-one years of emotion and love.

'Would you like to see him?' she asked.

Did she really have to ask? Did she think that I wouldn't want to see him? I couldn't speak. I just cried down the phone. All she must have heard was unintelligible sobbing.

'Of course I want to see him,' I said at last, so softly that she had to ask me to repeat it. 'Yes, of course I want to see my son.'

Sally went on to tell me that Jack had read my letter and told his father that he wanted to see me as soon as was possible. His father wasn't best pleased to hear this but had said that we could meet once, just once, and then it would be over.

I should have backed out then. I should have realised that once wasn't going to be enough, that I would want more than one meeting with my son. But I didn't.

'When does he want us to meet?' I asked quickly, as though if I waited he might change his mind. 'When will I see him?'

'Next Wednesday.' She said it as though it was a normal arrangement between two people, as though this happened every day of the week. Next Wednesday? Only a few days away!

'Yes, that's fine,' I heard a voice say. My voice. Surprisingly calm. Surprisingly together. I didn't feel calm or together, but my voice had spoken.

When I put the phone down, I couldn't stop shaking. Lucy sat and held me. She was so happy for me and, I think, for herself. She hoped that one day she would meet her half-brother, the child she had known about all of her life. But for now, this was mine. I didn't want to share any of it. I was going to see my son. Be reunited with the baby I had had to give up twenty-two years ago.

When my husband came home, I told him. I rang Melissa, the only other person in my life who had seen my baby, had shared a few precious weeks with him. I tried to stay calm, tried not to be too optimistic. For a while, the old fears came back into my life, from way back there. Fears that something would stop this from happening. I even wondered, that night in my bed, whether this was real. Could it have just been a dream? Had that phone call really happened? Of course I had always hoped and prayed that one day I would see him again. But hope and prayer had not often come through for me. Could I possibly be that lucky? I had a good marriage, a man who loved me just for me, I had two healthy daughters and I was free from my past. So wasn't I being a little selfish expecting more? Should I not have been content with what I had?

But God must have been listening. Perhaps not twenty-two years ago, but some time between then and now.

The next few days were like a dream. I asked for the day off work, and when my boss asked why, I told him.

'I'm going to see my son,' I said in a small voice, afraid that if I voiced it any louder, it wouldn't be true.

'I didn't know you had a son,' he said, surprised. 'I thought you only had the girls.'

I told him the whole sorry story and he just stood there, staring at me. At first I thought he was angry with me – for what, I didn't know. But he wasn't. He came over and put his arm around my shoulder and smiled.

'Go for it, girl,' he said in a strong voice. 'You go for it and enjoy.'

I shopped for a new dress. I had to look right. I wasn't sure what looking wrong was, but I had to look right. I chose a navy-blue fitted dress that didn't make me look too matronly but also didn't make me look too young. I wasn't dressing for a date; I was dressing to see my son.

The day came. I couldn't eat and hadn't slept the previous night. This was no ordinary Wednesday. This was a huge Wednesday.

We were to meet him, my son, in another town, on neutral ground. Daniel drove me because I couldn't have driven myself if I'd wanted to. We were taken upstairs into an office and sat talking to the social worker, or rather she was talking to us. Suddenly I knew he was in the building. I don't know how, but I knew.

'He's here,' I said quietly. 'I know he's here.'

As the door opened, I looked up. There he was. My beautiful son. Standing right in front of me.

I couldn't move, I couldn't stand, but I looked at him. It was the strangest feeling ever. He looked like both my daughters, like a boy with all of their features blended into one wonderful young man. He was slightly taller than Lucy, who was the taller of my daughters and taller than me, and his hair was the same dark, dark brown as my daughters' hair. He was wearing smart jeans and what looked like a new casual shirt. And suddenly, he was standing right there. My son. My Jack. I still couldn't speak. The air in the room was charged with raw emotion. You could feel it, almost touch it.

He didn't look at me, not at first. He looked at the social worker, he looked at my husband, but he didn't look at me. What if he doesn't like me? What if he thinks this is a mistake?

The social worker walked him over to where I was sitting. Daniel stood up and they shook hands, these two much-loved people in my life. And then he was there. Right in front of me, his mother.

What do you say to someone you lost a lifetime ago? I didn't know, I couldn't speak. So I said nothing. He sat down at my side and told me his name.

I know! I gave it to you. Of course I know your name!

I had made up a photo album, starting with images of my life in the present: my house, my husband and my dog. I showed this to him, explaining who and what everything was. Then we moved on to the pages that held photos of his sisters and he began to cry.

'I've never looked at a picture and seen myself looking back,' he said between the tears. 'I have never seen any similarities with me.'

I wanted to hold him, wanted to hold him so close that he would never leave. But I couldn't. I was too afraid. Afraid for myself and afraid for him. I mustn't touch him. Touching would be too painful. I felt I couldn't get that close.

I had made his father a promise that this would be a one-off meeting and then I would disappear out of my son's life forever.

Again. I had made a stupid, stupid promise. So I couldn't touch him and then let him go again.

I sat there, while he cried.

I then moved on to a photo of myself when I was pregnant with him. And then one of the only ones I had of him as a baby, before he was taken away.

He gasped and grabbed my hand. It was as though time had stopped. He was there, looking at me with the same beautiful blue eyes that had held my gaze the day he was born. We didn't speak; there was no need. We sat and held hands. I couldn't cry. What must he have thought? I hadn't cried about him and my loss for years. I had trained myself not to cry. His birth and losing him had been boxed away and was so tightly shut that I could only open it a little.

So I didn't cry. I just sat there telling him anything that he needed to know.

After what only seemed like minutes but also seemed like a lifetime, the social worker said that she had to shut the office. She had opened the rooms we were meeting in and had to return the key to the caretaker. I realised with a shock that it was almost midnight. We went outside and Daniel offered to drive my son home, but he said no. We were still holding hands and I tried to say goodnight. Suddenly he was in my arms. In the arms that had ached for him. The arms that should never have let him go. He was in my arms, where he belonged, and he started crying.

'Please take me with you,' he begged.

I should have held on to him. Held on and never let go. I know that now. Oh, how I have regretted that night. Regretted keeping a promise. A promise that was impossible to keep. I should have taken this beautiful young man home with me, where he should always have been – but I didn't.

I didn't, because I had made a promise.

'You have to go home,' I said. 'I promised your dad.' I tried to loosen his grip on my shoulders. I couldn't look at him. He was still sobbing.

Did he think I didn't want him? That I didn't care? I don't know. I did know that I had to hold on to my emotions, that somehow I had to be strong whilst he was falling apart in front of my eyes. It was one of the hardest things I had ever done. I just knew that I had to keep my promise.

In my naïvety, I thought that if I let him go home to his father, then his father would let us meet again. That he would see I wasn't a threat and realise how much it meant to his son, my son. I told Jack this and eventually he let go. My heart was breaking in two. No one could see it. I thought they might hear it. This isn't what I planned. This wasn't how it was supposed to be.

He asked if he could ring me later. I said that if it was OK with his dad, of course he could. Really what I wanted to say was 'Ring me, please ring me.'

Still shaking, and feeling very sick, I watched for the second time in my life as a social worker walked away with my son.

That night had been the best and the worst night of my life. When you make a memory, you don't just box away the good; you box away the good, the bad and the ugly. The good was having a beautiful baby boy, the bad was the grief and pain of having to give him up, the ugly, well that was everything else that happened around that awful painful time. And here on this night, everything came flooding back.

I don't remember the journey home. I do remember that when we arrived I was shivering and feeling very ill. I hadn't had a panic attack so that was a relief, but now I felt terrible. Lucy greeted us and wanted to know everything, but she could see that I wasn't up to talking and went to bed.

The following day I was exhausted. It felt like a dream, but the pain I was feeling was very real. It felt as it had felt when I had lost my baby son all those years ago. A pain so huge that it took over my whole being. I felt bereft, just as I had before, certain that last night was all I was going to have. One evening, one precious evening, where I was unable to speak, unable to tell Jack how I felt. Where I was not able to reach out and hold my son and keep him there. My arms had held him but my heart I kept at bay. I knew I couldn't take this pain again.

A day went by, and then another, and then the phone rang. 'Is that Cassie?' he asked. 'Is that you?'

I stood in disbelief; he was on the end of the line. The child I had once lost and thought I had lost again was at the end of the phone. What should I do? I mustn't blow it. I mustn't put him off.

'Yes, it's me. Where are you?' I asked, again quite calm. I don't know where that calm came from. But I was calm.

He told me that he was at work and would like to meet me that evening. Was that OK?

OK? Try and stop me. I didn't know what else to say in that call but yes. I think I kept it short so that he couldn't change his mind. My voice was calm but my heart and mind were racing.

We were to meet at the local railway station. He had broken his wrist and couldn't drive. I was trying not to think of the promise that I had made; I couldn't give up this chance. So I went to meet him.

I saw him come out of the station door and my heart said run to him. My heart said, take him in your arms and never let him go. But I couldn't listen to my heart. Couldn't take the risk.

I stayed in the car.

I called him over and he got in beside me. Nobody spoke at first. I suppose we were both as nervous as each other. We decided to go to a nearby pub, in an area that had been a favourite place of mine as a child. I told him this and wasn't ready for what he said next.

'Mum and Dad used to bring me here in the holidays. I came here a lot as a boy.' He said it as though it was no big deal. But it was. It was a very big deal! This was one of my places. Somewhere I still came to, to think and look into my memory box. He was telling me that he had come here many times as a child. That he had come here with his parents.

How could we both have visited the same place and I not have known? Why didn't we meet? How cruel is fate when it goes against you? I didn't know how to react to this earth-shattering bit of insight into his life.

'What kind of childhood did you have?' I asked, as if I were asking how his day had been.

He told me about his sister, about how his mum had been a worrier, a very anxious parent, sometimes too anxious. He told me of an incident when he was about eight years old when he almost drowned.

I should have been there to help you, I thought. Why wasn't I there?

By this stage I was beyond wanting answers. I couldn't take any more of his life, his far-away-from-me life. I had to change the subject; this was far too painful.

'How did your mum die?' My mouth spoke these words while my head was trying desperately to move on to something neutral, something that didn't keep reminding me that he had a life before that night. A life that I had played no part in.

He told me.

'It must have been a terrible time for you,' I said. 'I'm so sorry that you had to go through that.'

But I'm still here. I'm always here for you. I'm your mum.

My heart was once again breaking as I watched this young man cry. Crying for the woman who had taken my place all those years ago. The woman he knew as his mum.

After he had told me of her death, he wanted to talk about me, about my life. Not about his birth, not about what had happened, but about my life. And so I told him. I told him about meeting and marrying Daniel, about the book I had written, about my pets. I sensed that tonight was not the right time to talk about his sisters, his birth and his adoption. That was fine with me. I wanted this to be a time for us.

At the end of an evening that was, in fact, quite long but seemed so short, I took him back to the station. Although it was late and dark, I still had the roof down on my little convertible car.

He stood up in the car, towering above me, and said, 'Thanks for coming, thanks for seeing me. Can we do this again some time?'

Of course we could, of course we will, I told him, and he said goodnight and made his way into the railway station.

I wanted to scream out for him to come back and we would go home together, but I didn't. I was seeing him and that had to be enough. I didn't want to spoil anything.

We met on our own once more and then he asked to meet his sisters. It was arranged that he would come to our house and Lucy insisted on going to meet him at the station. I watched them walking up the road hand in hand, very slowly, deep in conversation, and my heart lurched at such a wonderful, unbelievable sight. The daughter who was becoming my best friend and the son who had been lost from our lives were walking along as though it was the most natural thing in the world.

That evening was strange. The atmosphere in the room was almost dreamlike. At first Melissa didn't say a word. I could see tears in her eyes, but she didn't say anything. Lucy and Jack were already very relaxed in each other's company. We talked about their childhoods, their hobbies. There were a few funny moments to recall and eventually everyone was talking freely. At the end of this visit, Jack asked to talk to me on his own.

'I'm so glad you let me meet them,' he said, slightly tearful. 'I've always wondered if I had any brothers or sisters. I was never told.'

Why on earth hadn't he been told, I wondered?

'I knew nothing, nothing about you, why I wasn't able to stay with you or anything. Just that you didn't want me.' He was looking at the floor.

Didn't want you? How could they have said that? How dare they?

'Did you get the poem I wrote?' I asked, not wanting to hear the answer. 'And the elephant from your pram? Did they give you the clothes I bought for you to go to them in?' My voice was getting louder, perhaps a bit hysterical. 'You must have had those? They promised.'

I knew before he shook his head. They hadn't.

This news felt like a real betrayal. The one thing that had kept me sane after the awful time when he was taken away from me had been the promise they made to me. Now, I found they had betrayed me. Betrayed Jack. He had grown up thinking I hadn't wanted him. That I didn't love him.

'I think we need some time together so that I can explain everything,' I said softly. 'So that I can tell you how it really was.'

And then I said it. Said the one thing that I had wanted him to know since the very day I had given him life.

'I have always loved you. I loved you even before you were born. I have always regretted the day I lost you and will regret it until the day I die.'

This beautiful young man leaned forward and took me in his arms.

That's when I cried.

'It's OK,' he said, 'it's OK. I'm here now and I will always be here for you.'

I couldn't take in what he was saying. I should have just let him continue and to hell with anyone else. Promises? What promises? Did they keep theirs to me? No. I should have just let him carry on. But I am my own worst enemy.

'What about your dad?' I asked. 'He doesn't want you seeing me, does he?'

'Blood's thicker than water. You're my mum,' was all he said.

That's all I heard. I was his mum.

After that evening I allowed myself to hope that his dad would be OK with us staying in touch. After all, I was no threat to him. All I wanted was to get to know my son.

We spent more time together. I gave him the poem that he should have had whilst growing up and I told him my side of what had happened when he was a baby. I was careful not to malign his adoptive parents. I thought he understood. I thought we were OK.

This went on for about a year. He rang now and again, even asking for 'Mum' when my husband answered. This was joy to my ears. But after a while I realised that I had become a secret. He hadn't told his father about me. For all he knew, we had only met once. I should have left it at that. I should have been satisfied with what I had. But I wasn't. My life had been haunted by secrets, and very few of them were good. When I asked Jack about it he said it was the only way he could keep seeing me, ringing me. His father had forbidden him to have contact with any of us and my son had agreed.

I suppose I thought at that time that I deserved all of this. I had let my son down when he was a baby, so I deserved it. We kept in touch for a while and then he just stayed away. No visits. No phone calls, nothing.

Melissa still saw him, and I was pleased for her, but he had no contact with Lucy. I suppose because she was still living with me, this would have been too difficult, but I was pleased for Melissa. Jealous, yes, but pleased for them both. A few years went by and thoughts of this young man, my son, out there having a life without me, made things worse for me. When I thought about the baby that had been taken from me, those thoughts were painful enough. But now that I knew Jack and could picture him, this was much worse.

He married and went on to have a child, a baby girl, my grandchild. A child I could never know. It felt that I was being punished for letting him go all those years before. I hadn't had a choice but I wondered how much he had believed of what I had told him.

I should have left it there. I met him, I loved him, I lost him again. I should have left it.

But I didn't.

One day, a year after I had heard about his daughter, I rang his home. His wife answered. She said she understood why I had rung but wasn't sure if he would speak to me. Jack's father had found out about us and he had again forbidden his son, my son, from contacting me. This wasn't enough for me. I had to speak to him. I was still hoping that as God had listened and I had seen my son again, didn't he owe it to me to let me make it right? Would he really have allowed us to meet just to take this away from me again? Hadn't I suffered enough?

I was only thinking of myself at that time. I desperately needed to make things better. I wasn't thinking of anyone else, so perhaps I deserved what happened next.

His wife promised to ask him to ring me and at 3.30 that afternoon the phone rang. I was almost tempted not to answer because then I wouldn't have to know what he was going to say.

'Is that you, Cassie?' he asked in a voice I hadn't heard before.

Why not 'Mum'? 'Yes, it's me. Are you OK?' I croaked down the receiver. 'Did you get my message?' Of course he had; that's why he was ringing.

'It's difficult,' he said. 'I don't know how to say this.'

'You know you can tell me anything,' I whispered, while thinking please don't say it. Don't say the words that will mean goodbye.

'You know it's always been difficult with my dad and you. I had to make a choice and I have grown up knowing him and not knowing you.'

I didn't speak, I couldn't speak.

He went on calmly. 'There's no room in my life for you or your daughters.'

By this time I had started to blubber down the phone. 'Don't say that, you can't say that. I'm your mum,' I cried, not sure he could understand me through the tears and sobs.

'Look,' he said, as though he were talking about the price of bread, 'I don't need you. Everything I need is in my life now. The past has to stay where it belongs. In the past.'

I was a wreck: crying, sobbing, begging him to think again. I don't know what I expected. Perhaps I thought that his saying about blood being thicker than water would come into his mind and he would stop. Stop this awful conversation that was to leave me broken. Again.

But he didn't.

His voice became firmer; he was adamant that this would be the last conversation that we would have. He had made his choice. He would keep his promise to his dad. He wouldn't see me again.

He put the phone down.

I was on the floor, crying the tears that I had held on to for many years. Tears for the loss of my baby and tears that I had held onto since I met Jack again. That's where Daniel found me.

I blamed myself. I was so afraid of making a mistake, so wanting to get it right, that I got it wrong. I should have forgotten everyone but the two of us. I should have followed my heart. At that first meeting, when Jack asked me to take him home with him, I should have done it. At the second meeting, when he came out of the station, I should have run up and taken him in my arms. I shouldn't have honoured my promise to his dad. My beloved son, whom I lost so many years before, must have felt rejected: totally rejected, in his eyes, for a second time. I should have been true to my feelings and showered him with all the love I felt, instead of holding back and waiting to see what he wanted. I blamed myself, just as I had always taken the blame for everything in my life. Somehow it must be my fault. I understood and accepted that he was loyal to his dad, but I could have handled the whole reunion so much better than I did. I wish with all my heart that I had.

Melissa said Jack had told her that he never really understood why I hadn't kept him when he was a baby. I think he blamed me, found it hard to forgive me. She didn't think he really understood any of it. And now I had lost him again.

It took a long time for me to accept what had happened. I took a lot longer to come back from this pain, this hurt. But come back I did. Eventually.

When the pain got less, I carried on my life with my husband and daughters. I think I was still growing, gaining my strength, learning about myself. I was happy, yes. I suppose I thought I could have been happier with Jack in my life, but I will never know.

Acceptance of Jack's choice eventually came and I was happy. I loved my job and enjoyed my life. My marriage was wonderful, Daniel was wonderful and Lucy had become my best friend. Melissa had moved away and had her own life by this time, but we were still close.

Why did I ever think that this calm, comfortable period would last? Yes, I had changed and I was stronger than I had ever been in my life. After the last hurt, I began to think that nothing could ever hurt me again. But I was wrong. Oh so wrong. My past was about to come back and cause me more pain that I had thought possible. Pain that would bring everything out in the open, for all the world to see.

And this time I told!

Chapter Twenty-three

I heard that Gwen, Uncle Bill's wife, was in a rest home and decided to visit her. This lady had been kind to me in the past and I now realised that she needn't have been. I had met her a few years before in the shopping centre where we lived and she had seemed so pleased to see me that I decided to contact her and say I was sorry for the pain she endured at the hands of my mum and Bill. I wanted it all brought out into the open at last.

When I arrived at the home, I was told that she had dementia and wouldn't know who I was, but that was OK. It wasn't important. In fact, it might be for the best. She was asleep when I got to her bedside. She was tiny and frail, but she looked at peace. I couldn't help thinking about how hard it must have been for her when I was born and she had been told I was her husband's child. Although I knew she couldn't hear me, I sat down and whispered how sorry I was for all the pain that my mother had caused her. Then I left, comforted by the fact I had made my peace.

I did tell, I did

A couple of years later when I saw the notice in the local paper saying that she had died, I wanted to go to her funeral. I didn't want to upset anyone, but I just wanted to be there.

On the day of the funeral, I arrived just before the service started. In my naïvety, I believed that if I went in at the back of the crematorium chapel I could quietly slip away through that same door, before the mourners came out. Stupid me. I forgot that, because of the steady flow of services, once in the chapel, the only way out was through the other door, at the front. That meant following the family mourners and friends out into the memorial gardens.

A few months earlier we had moved to a new house and Lucy had changed schools. One day she brought home a new friend called Anita and we started talking about the area we lived in, then I asked her last name. I couldn't believe what she replied. Her surname was a very unusual one, the name that had destroyed my childhood, the surname of my abuser. His name.

Uncle Bill had had four sons, one of them Steve, the boy I had fallen in love with at the age of seventeen. This could be Steve's daughter.

I was careful not to show how shocked I was at the revelation as I asked the name of her dad. I hope the relief didn't show when she named one of Steve's younger brothers. Still, it meant that Anita was related to us. And Gwen, Uncle Bill's wife, was her grandmother.

I went to the funeral of this new friend's grandmother, my godmother. I don't know why I thought I could get away without being seen. When the service was over, I had no choice but to follow the mourners, the family and friends, my half-brothers, out into the gardens. I didn't want to look for Steve, the young love of my life, I didn't want to. But I did. I recognised the two older boys because one looked just like his father, and I shivered with memories.

At first I didn't see the boy I had planned to marry all those years ago. I decided that this was for the best and started to make my way to the car. Then I heard a voice: 'Hello, Cassie! What are you doing here?' It was my daughter's new friend Anita.

Before I could answer, she called her father over and introduced us. He was the youngest of Bill's sons and had just been a child when the truth had come out about my parentage.

'Did you know my mum?' he asked in all innocence. 'Were you on the staff at the home?'

If only I had left it at that. If only my honesty had kept quiet and I had left it there. But I didn't.

'You don't know who I am, do you?' I asked this man who was grieving for his mum. 'I'm Cassie.' I knew my voice sounded tiny, afraid. 'Cassie, Kath's daughter.'

I'm not sure what the look he gave me meant. It wasn't hostile, it wasn't even unfriendly, but I'm not sure what it was.

'Have you seen him?' he asked, without having to give 'him' a name. 'I'll go and get him.'

Before I could protest, he ran over to where his brother stood and brought him to me. Suddenly, Steve was in front of me. He didn't speak, I didn't speak. We just looked at each other. I could see from his expression that he didn't have a clue who I was. But he wouldn't have. The old Cassie had gone, the Cassie with the pain, the hurt and the grief. In front of him stood a woman who looked nothing like the old me. When we last met, that awful day when we had said goodbye, I had long black hair; I was still haunted by my past and at that time by a confused present. I was different now, more confident; I had shortish blonde hair and was dressed in a dark suit. I had given birth to three children. I had changed.

'It's me,' I said tentatively. 'It's me, Cassie.'

I will never forget the look on his face. I wasn't sure whether he was going to burst into tears. It was a look that said so much but said nothing at all.

'Where's your hair?' he asked. 'Where's your lovely hair?'

It didn't need an answer and I wasn't going to give one.

He looked at my face, by now tear-stained, and said, 'Oh, come here.'

I moved towards him, he held me in his arms and we both cried. The past came flooding back, bringing with it the pain and hurt of that day long ago. But we were different people now. Nothing could take away our memories; nothing could take away the horror of that discovery which caused us such sadness. But we were different now.

After a while he released me and said, 'You must meet my wife, Pamela,' and I was OK with that. He went over to a pretty lady in a smart suit, who was talking with some other mourners, and brought her by the hand over to me.

'This is Kath's daughter, Cassie.'

She looked at me closely. 'So you're Cassie,' she said. 'I've lived with your ghost for all of my marriage.'

I didn't know what to say, didn't want to say anything.

Steve smiled and said he was glad we had met again. I asked if his older brothers would see me. I wanted to tell them on behalf of my mother that I was sorry. Steve said that it wasn't the time, because they were obviously still very upset at their mother's death. He promised to ask them after a while if they would meet me, but he wasn't optimistic. They had been very close to their mum and were very protective. Both the older boys had been young lads when I was born and the affair came to light; they had seen what it had done to their mum, so he wasn't optimistic. He asked me for my telephone number, I gave it to him and then I left. Although I felt I was intruding, neither of these younger boys said I was. They both agreed that I had a right to be there, as their half-sister.

When I arrived home, I felt shattered. I hadn't expected any of what had happened. But it felt good. I had often wondered how it would be if we met again, my young love and I, and now I knew. We would be OK. We were OK. Warmth and love had surrounded us standing in that beautiful sad garden, love for each other that hadn't died but had changed through necessity and time. We now had the love of a brother and sister, and that felt good. Life had been enhanced once again.

But it wouldn't last.

Steve phoned me the next day and asked to see me. Of course I said yes and we arranged to meet the following evening at his house. I was nervous and my husband offered to take me there.

Daniel was keen to meet this person from my past whom he had heard so much about. He still didn't know much about my childhood, and he certainly didn't know about the horrendous sexual abuse I had suffered at the hands of Steve's father. I hadn't told him, as I hadn't told anyone. Except Mum, and then Peter.

As we arrived, Pamela, my half-brother's wife, was leaving. She smiled warmly at me and said she would be back later, that she had a meeting to attend. I was relieved to see her smile. That meant she didn't have a problem with me.

Steve, Daniel and I had a coffee and started to talk about the past. Steve told me that none of Bill's sons had attended his funeral. They had hated the way he treated their mum and had all fallen out with him before his death.

I don't know if he saw the look on my face when my abuser's name was mentioned, but he saw something.

'I'm sorry, Cassie,' he said kindly, 'I know how you loved him, but he was a bad man.' He came over and crouched at my feet. He sounded angry, angry and hurt.

I started crying uncontrollably. Before he could say any more, I put my hand on his arm. 'I didn't love him,' I gasped through my tears. 'I didn't love him.'

'But we all thought …'

I was suffocating under years of pretence and lies and at last the truth burst out. 'He raped me,' I said. 'He raped me.' My voice was sinking to an almost inaudible whisper.

Daniel tried to move over to comfort me, but Steve put his arm out to stop him. It was he who held me – Steve, with his own demons, his own pain and hurt, held me and cried with me for what seemed like forever.

Steve really hated our abuser, the man who had treated his mother so badly. He said my revelation had made him angrier than he would have thought possible. He knew how badly my mum had treated me, but he had never known that the evil man had also so cruelly and horrendously abused me. He told of the hatred the whole family felt towards my mum. It was hard to hear about the terrible pain that these two people, my parents, had caused to Steve, someone I loved.

At the end of that evening, I was feeling a furious anger that I hadn't thought I was capable of. I wanted to see my abuser face to face. The fact that he was dead had always been a comfort to me because his death had removed the fear and terror I had felt, but now I wished he were here, alive, so that I could somehow make him pay for the pain he had inflicted on us, his victims.

I was also worried about the way this horror had been blurted out in front of my husband. He knew now. He knew the whole horrible everything. What would he think? Would he still love me? Please let him still love me.

When we got home, I asked Daniel how he felt and he held me and reassured me that nothing from my past would ever make him change the way he felt about me. With that love, that reassurance, we went to bed and tried to put the evening where it belonged, in the past. But for me it was still very raw.

I couldn't forget, couldn't leave it alone, but I didn't know what I could do with it either. I just knew I had to do something with this horrendous information. The anger I felt towards Mum had no bounds. I believe that this strength made it possible for me to take the action I took next. It didn't matter what I did now or what repercussions there might be, because nothing could make this right and nothing would take away the wrong.

I decided to write a letter to my mother. It wasn't difficult; it didn't take long. I just sat and poured my heart out in a letter.

I started by telling her about Gwen's funeral and about my feelings of guilt on her, my mother's behalf. I told her how I had felt betrayed as a child after I told her that Uncle Bill had sexually abused me and she had done nothing. I reminded her of how she shouted and screamed at me that it wasn't true, that I was a liar. I went on to tell her that this sexual abuse continued throughout my growing years and how I had to endure it on my own. Terrified and alone. I told her that her affair with Bill had caused other people tremendous pain and hurt and had left me with a legacy that was hard to bear. I reminded her of the tranquillisers I had taken and the reason they were first given to me. How at first, before I knew the dangers, they had helped me to get on with my life and shut the boxes that held the terrible truth. She knew how dependent I had become on them and I reminded her how she turned her back on me, once again, when I was going through withdrawal.

As I wrote this letter, I cried. Cried for the child who was me, little Cassie who had grown up in a loveless childhood, a childhood that was filled with horror, abuse, cruelty and loneliness. I cried for the boy I had loved, whom I should never have loved, for the pain and sadness that she, my mother, and her lover had caused to him and his family. I cried, remembering the times my dad, my beloved dad, had suffered mental cruelty at her hands. Lots and lots of tears. The letter continued to ask her why. Why hadn't she believed me about Uncle Bill? Why had she not wanted me? Why couldn't she love me?

I'm not sure why I wrote this long, long letter. I needed to put this to bed, leave it in the past, but not before she knew. Not before I had told her that I knew the whole truth now.

I posted the letter before I had a chance to change my mind. I posted it and tried to forget what I had discovered, forget the truth.

But life isn't that easy.

I wasn't allowed to forget.

A few days later I arrived home to find a policeman at my door.

'We've had a complaint,' he said, 'a complaint about you having sent malicious mail, threatening letters.'

Daniel was at home and we both looked at each other, speechless.

The police officer continued, 'You wrote a letter to your mother recently?'

I replied that I had, but that it was a private matter.

He took a letter out of his folder and handed it to me. 'Is this the letter?' he asked.

I took the offending pieces of paper out of his hand and told him it was. It was the letter I had written to her.

'We were called to her flat because of the distress it caused her receiving it,' he said.

Distress? She didn't know the meaning of the word. I wasn't sure what to say. I explained to him that I had sent it because of some new information I had heard a few days previously. I was hurting and I wanted her to know the pain she had caused me. I felt that I had to tell her what I knew and show how it made me feel. I never meant to hurt her.

'We have to follow up every complaint. It's our duty,' he said kindly. 'She made the complaint but then she wasn't very happy about letting me read the letter.'

I don't suppose she was. She hadn't reckoned on that when she called the police. Now others would hear the truth and she wouldn't like that at all.

'So what happens now?' I asked him.

'Nothing,' he said. 'Nothing at all. I read the letter and because she insisted that I take it further and show a senior officer, I had to carry out her wishes. The superintendent I showed it to agreed with me, that the letter is the pouring out of a daughter's pain to her mother.' He looked at me with such warmth that my fears dissipated. 'I have told your mother to stay away from you, not to contact you in any way, and I suggest you do the same.'

He didn't need to say this.

I never thought for one moment that Mum would reply to my letter. And I certainly didn't think that she would stoop this low. But the complaint had backfired on her. She had been seen for who she was, warts and all. To have someone else read what she had been accused of must have been very painful for her, the woman who cared so much about what people would think. But I didn't care. She had opened this up to people outside the safety of her family. She had made our secrets public, not me. I had been warned as a child never to tell. This time I definitely told!

When I'd told her about Uncle Bill's abuse back at the age of seven, maybe, just maybe, my childish explanations were unconvincing. Now I had set it out unequivocally, in black and white, you'd think any normal mother would have been horrified and racked with guilt that they hadn't protected their child. But mine wasn't any normal mother. Far from rushing round to apologise and condemn the man who had made my childhood a living nightmare, she tried to have me arrested. She was a cold, heartless woman.

Writing the letter didn't make me feel any better. I didn't feel released from my past, but I was able to move a little further away from the memories. I had to, to survive. My childhood and young adulthood had caused me so much pain that the only way I had been able to continue living was to take the tranquillisers and leave the horrors of the abuse, the betrayal and the loneliness in the boxes I had made for them. Leave them boxed up and throw away the key. But now the boxes had been ripped open and all the contents strewn at my feet. I couldn't avoid them any more, but I didn't have to look at them closely. I knew they were there – I was aware of that every day – but I didn't have to look at them.

In August 1996 my husband, youngest daughter and our menagerie all moved to Wales and I decided to go back to college and train to be a counsellor in Cognitive Behaviour

Therapy. It was tough doing the course as it forced me to analyse many more issues from my past, but eventually, just before the new millennium, I gained my Masters degree.

At the graduation ceremony, as I walked up on stage to receive my scroll, I was nervous about tripping over in front of the watching crowd. And there was something else as well: I was scared that I would be found out to be unworthy. I was the little girl who was unloved and unwanted. Everyone there would somehow know where I had come from and see through me, see the real me.

Then suddenly I realised the truth.

Of course they would. This *was* me. This was the Cassie I had always wanted to be. The Cassie who had struggled through childhood and earlier times, without being able to show who she really was. This is who they would see – me! And it was OK. For the first time ever, I was beginning to like myself.

It was a wonderful moment, a moment when I knew that life was good. That God was listening after all.

Epilogue

I hadn't seen or heard from my mother since the letter episode, which was fine by me. Or so I thought. But one Christmas I sent her a card. I don't know why I did that or what I thought would happen. I hadn't expected a reply but when an envelope arrived with her writing on it, I was excited. I thought she had sent me a card in return. I hoped that she wanted contact with me. Why did I still keep hoping?

I tore the envelope open excitedly and there it was – the card I had sent to her, returned. Returned with a note saying that she had no daughter called Cassie. She had all the family that was hers, all the family she wanted, in her life.

She hadn't changed. I threw the card in the bin.

Some of the old issues kept coming back because I kept inviting them. I decided to let go of any hopes about her and get on with the rest of my life.

I only saw Mum one more time, in the summer of 2003. Tom rang to let me know she was seriously ill in hospital and, although Daniel cautioned me against it, I decided to visit her to say my goodbyes. When I walked in I peered round the ward, looking for her. Where was this huge influence on my life? Where was this formidable woman who had hated me so much?

A nurse came over and pointed to a bed where a frail, grey-haired woman was lying. It was her. The woman who couldn't love me, the woman who hadn't believed me or helped me, the woman who was my mother.

She saw Daniel and me walking towards her bed. At first I don't think she realised who I was, then, as recognition dawned, she looked behind me and saw my husband. She had an audience, someone to play-act to.

'Oh Cassie,' she cried, 'my darling Cassie, I've been so ill, so unhappy.'

She reached for me, stretching her arms up as I bent down to her bed. Still acting after all these years!

'How are you?' I asked in a neutral voice. 'Are you feeling any better?'

'I am now, dear,' she said using her small poor-me voice. 'I am now you're here.' She looked over at Daniel. 'Thank you for bringing her,' she said.

'It's OK, I'd do anything for my girl,' replied the man who loved me, the man who supported me in everything I did.

'She's only half yours,' retorted this woman in her sick bed. 'The other half will always be mine.'

It sounded cruel and possessive, not a motherly kind of sentiment, but one of ownership that I didn't like the sound of.

We stayed and talked with her for a while but all she could do was moan about everything: her treatment in the hospital, my other siblings, how seldom people visited her. It was all a game to make people feel sorry for her. She had always played games with me and she was still playing games now.

'Promise me you'll come to my funeral,' she asked before we left, and so I agreed that I would.

A few weeks later I got a phone call from Tom's wife to say that Mum had died that morning. My reaction surprised me. I screamed and collapsed on the floor sobbing, great awful sobs that wracked my body. Why was I crying? She'd never loved me, I knew she hadn't. What did it matter?

But I wasn't crying for her. I wasn't crying for losing a mum. How could I cry for something I'd never had? No, I was crying for me. For the lost opportunities, for lost maybes, but most of all for lost hope. Hope that one day she would explain her inactions; explain why she had treated me the way she had. That one day she would say she was sorry and that she loved me. But now, this day would never happen. Now hope had died forever. I felt bereft, yes, but not for her. My tears were for the child I had been and for myself.

I kept my promise to Mum and went to her funeral. There were only eight of us there – a family saying goodbye to whatever the being in the coffin had meant to us. I didn't want to say anything except goodbye – goodbye to the woman who had been my mother and goodbye to my past.

When we got home that evening, I felt somehow free. Free from the past, free to move on to the next part of my life. A

I did tell, I did

huge burden had been lifted from my shoulders. And now that hope had gone, I felt acceptance. Acceptance that she had never loved or wanted me. Acceptance that she had never protected me, that she wasn't sorry. Acceptance that I would never know in full the reasons for her hatred of me.

I could go back to being happy. No, I wasn't loved as a child. But I know I am loved now, and ultimately that is all that matters.

Acknowledgements

Special thanks to Gill Paul, my patient and sensitive editor, for helping me through the hardest parts and understanding my need to be honest.

To Carole Tonkinson of HarperCollins for seeing the book's potential on first draft. And thanks to Kate Latham, also of HarperCollins, for her kindness and understanding. Thank you also to Andrew Lownie, my literary agent.

I would like to say thank you to Peter for his belief in me and his zany sense of humour in our numerous e-mails. But most of all I want to say thank you to my wonderful husband and friend, for his love, endurance and endless support not only for now but for the past twenty-two years. A special thank you to my daughters for their love and support, especially my youngest daughter and best friend, for her love, patience and endless reminders that I am Me and Me is good.

The last thank you is for my half-brother who, when told of my book, encouraged me by saying, 'Go for it, love.' So I have taken his advice and gone for it!